Religion, Power, Politics

Religion, Power, Politics

Konrad Raiser

*Translated from the German
by Stephen Brown*

RELIGION, POWER, POLITICS
Copyright © 2013 WCC Publications. All rights reserved. Except for brief quotations in notices or reviews, no part of this book may be reproduced in any manner without prior written permission from the publisher. Write: publications@wcc-coe.org.

WCC Publications is the book publishing programme of the World Council of Churches. Founded in 1948, the WCC promotes Christian unity in faith, witness and service for a just and peaceful world. A global fellowship, the WCC brings together more than 349 Protestant, Orthodox, Anglican and other churches representing more than 560 million Christians in 110 countries and works cooperatively with the Roman Catholic Church.

Opinions expressed in WCC Publications are those of the authors.

Scripture quotations are from the New Revised Standard Version Bible, © copyright 1989 by the Division of Christian Education of the National Council of the Churches of Christ in the USA. Used by permission.

Author photo: World Council of Churches
Cover design: Adele Robey/Phoenix Graphics, Inc.
Book design and typesetting: 4 Seasons Book Design/Michelle Cook
ISBN: 978-2-8254-1599-3

World Council of Churches
150 route de Ferney, P.O. Box 2100
1211 Geneva 2, Switzerland
http://publications.oikoumene.org

Contents

Introduction	1
1. Religion and Politics in Conflict?	11
The Return of Religion to the Public Sphere	11
Religion and Politics: What Are We Talking About?	17
Religion and Politics in Premodern Societies	23
Redefining the Relationship between Religion and Politics in Modern Europe	29
Modernization and Secularization	32
Critique and the Further Development of Secularization Theory	36
2. Beyond Church and State	41
The Public Space: State and Politics	41
Religion in the Public Space: Europe	45
Public Religion in the United States of America	50
Public Religion in Postcolonial States	53
The Debate about Religious Freedom	58
3. Religion and Politics in Islam	61
The Return of Islam to the Political Stage	61
Dissolution of the Traditional Order and Reform Movements	70
The Question of Islamism	73
Islamic Perspectives for a New World Order	81
Future Perspectives	88

4. The Challenge of Fundamentalism	95
The Political Shift of Fundamentalism	99
Fundamentalism as a General Type of Political Religion	101
Fundamentalist Movements in World Religions	105
Fundamentalism and the Power of Religion in Society	112
5. Religion, Power, and Politics	119
Legitimacy Problems in the World of States	119
Order, Power, and Violence	122
Power, Law, and Morality	128
Political and Religious Action in the Public Space	134
Religions as Advocates for a Culture of Dialogue and Peace	138
Summary and Conclusion	149
Notes	153

Introduction

The relationship between religion and politics is currently the subject of heated debate, not only in academic books and essays, but also at conferences and in the programmes of political foundations. The debate has even reached the editorial pages of the major newspapers. This is astonishing, given the otherwise strictly secular character of public, and particularly political, discourse, at least within European societies. While public opinion as portrayed in the media was and still is prepared to accord religion a limited place within the public space, it nevertheless insists on a clear separation between religion and politics.

One of the catalysts for this unexpected and critical interest in the relationship between religion and politics has certainly been the debate about developments in the Muslim world dating from the Iranian Revolution of 1979 up to current militant forms of Islamism and the international terrorism that invokes them. This obliges us to reflect anew on the secular conception of the state and politics that our culture takes for granted. Our preconceptions are also challenged by the observation that despite the constitutional separation of church and state in the United States, conservative Christian positions have exercised a direct influence on government policy, and not only under the administration of President George W. Bush.

Moreover, there are many countries and regions in which religious traditions have become allied to ethnic and nationalist political movements and have been used to legitimize "identity politics."

Such tendencies have become stronger since the end of the Cold War and through the pressure of the process of globalization. As a result, many observers and commentators have concluded that religious differences and tensions are among the key reasons for the civil conflicts and disputes of recent decades. According to this view, religion is therefore above all a highly problematic factor in the political arena, and thus needs to be neutralized as far as possible and kept out of the political process.

Such a view has gained additional support from the theory of the American political scientist Samuel P. Huntington, who sees the ideological conflict between the two power blocs of the Cold War being replaced by a "clash of civilizations," in which a different religion is identified as being at the centre of the eight civilizations that he describes. The theory that he first presented in a 1993 essay and then three years later in a much-discussed book titled *The Clash of Civilizations and the Remaking of World Order* became, in retrospect, a "self-fulfilling prophecy" given the attacks of 11 September 2001 and the proclamation of the "War on Terror" that followed it.[1]

A response to Huntington's provocative thesis came from an unexpected quarter. In a speech to the General Assembly of the United Nations on 21 September 1998, the then president of the Islamic Republic of Iran, Seyed Mohammad Khatami, proposed that the year 2001 be declared the "Year of Dialogue among Civilizations." The Tübingen theologian Hans Küng had already been promoting his conviction that "there will be no peace among the nations without peace among the religions" in his lectures and in discussions at UNESCO. His efforts bore fruit in 1993 in the "Declaration Toward a Global Ethic" at the Second Parliament of the World's Religions in Chicago.[2] After the General Assembly of the United Nations had adopted Khatami's proposal, the then UN secretary-general, Kofi Annan, appointed a "group of eminent persons," including Küng and Richard von Weizsäcker, to draw up a report on the Dialogue of Cultures. The report was published in 2001 with the title *Crossing the Divide: Dialogue among Civilizations*.[3] It countered the theory of the clash of civilizations, based on the classical friend/enemy perspective, with a new paradigm for global relations based on dialogue and cooperation and guided by the affirmation of common values as formulated in the Declaration Toward a Global Ethic.

This is the background to the question being dealt with in this book as to whether religions are able to provide an autonomous and possibly even a constitutive contribution to building a new world order. This is linked to the wider question as to whether in the global context, and in what way, traditional perspectives on the role of religion and politics need to be revised and rethought. The starting point for this study is the observation that globalization has demonstrated the limits of the state-centred paradigm of the international order and has made urgent the development of forms of political governance that transcend the model of the nation-state, which is sovereign both internally and externally. The state-centred and secular understanding of politics is linked to a particular understanding of religious practice and to demands for the legal and institutional separation of religion and politics that are questionable in a global framework. It is the "return" of religion to national and global public space that points to fundamental problems of legitimacy in the "world of states." A world order that does not exist exclusively to balance the national interest of sovereign states, but is intended be in accordance with the intentions and interests of people and nations, needs, for the sake of its own legitimacy, to respect the values transmitted through the cultural and religious traditions of humanity and to translate them into general rules for human coexistence. The development of a global "rule of law" based on the universal application of human rights presupposes the creation of a "public space" within which religion and politics are able to deploy their distinct but interrelated power to become responsible for shaping a future world order.

The first chapter examines the historical development of the fraught relationship between religion and politics and the way each of them relates to power. It becomes clear that the secular understanding of politics and the increasing banishment of religion to the private sphere is the result of a historical process in Europe that is without parallel in other regions. The secularization theory based on this development and the assumption that there is a necessary connection between modernization and secularization must therefore be revised. Chapter 2 introduces the concept of the "public space" and sets out its consequences for understanding religion and politics. It examines the different forms of public religion in Europe, the United States of America, and in postcolonial states. The public space is the area of interaction between religion and politics and their respective forms of power. The fundamental significance of the principle of religious freedom is that it prescribes rules as protection both from the hegemonic claims of institutional politics and from attempts to establish religious or cultural domination. Chapter 3 traces the historical development of Islam and the current controversies about the relationship of religion and politics within Islam, and attempts to sketch out Islamic perspectives for a new world order by picking up the reform discourse within Islam and against the background of recent interreligious dialogue. Chapter 4 tackles the challenge of fundamentalism, which is not restricted to its Muslim form. It begins by examining the origins of Christian fundamentalism in the United States, then moves on to a more general analysis of fundamentalism as a form of "political" religion that has developed in the various religious traditions as a reaction to conflicts over modernization. The debate with fundamentalist movements underlines the need to critically reevaluate the power of religion in society and to develop new forms of the relationship between religion and politics that preserve the freedom and integrity of both of these dimensions and their significance for the life of society. This task is the focus of chapter 5, which, on the basis of what has gone before, concludes the study by attempting to redefine the interaction of religion and politics as far as the relationship between religion, power, and morality is concerned. The aim is to develop criteria for differentiating between political and religious action in the public space, given their simultaneous reciprocal relationship. In this context, religions have a particular responsibility to be advocates of a culture of dialogue and peace.

The starting point for this study has been the insight and conviction gained through Christian ecumenical and interreligious work that we need to give greater attention to the action of religious communities in the public space. A central concern for all religious traditions is the preservation of a sustainable order in which peoples and nations are able to coexist. They serve in all traditions as the "custodians" of the foundations and rules that maintain order and provide protection from chaos and self-destruction. This can be briefly demonstrated in the following three examples.

First, the declaration of a global ethic of the Parliament of the World's Religions is based on the "Golden Rule" that is present in all religious traditions as a basic norm for human coexistence and develops this principle in four "guidelines" or commitments:

- Commitment to a culture of nonviolence and respect for life;
- Commitment to a culture of solidarity and a just economic order;
- Commitment to a culture of tolerance and a life of truthfulness;
- Commitment to a culture of equal rights and partnership between men and women.[4]

Since then, in later meetings of the parliament, this basic orientation has been further developed and made more specific. Alongside this there is a range of suggestions for interreligious and intercultural cooperation in dialogue, to which reference is made in chapter 4.

Second, the triad of "Justice, Peace and the Integrity of Creation" affirmed in the Christian ecumenical discussion names the crucial values to which a new world order must be directed if it is to be viable and sustainable. At the World Convocation for Justice, Peace and the Integrity of Creation in Seoul in 1990, ten affirmations were formulated that developed these values,[5] gathering the harvest of more than four decades of ecumenical discussion. From the very beginning, "responsibility for the world" has been a central theme of the work of the World Council of Churches. In the first two decades following the founding assembly in Amsterdam (1948), efforts to prevent a nuclear confrontation between the two power blocs during the Cold War were at the forefront. In the course of decolonization, the issues of economic and social development and overcoming racism gained in importance. By the mid-1990s, at the latest, the issue of globalization and its consequences had moved to the centre of the discussion. There is no doubt that the search for a new world order has taken on a new urgency and quality for the churches because of the process of globalization.

Third, the Roman Catholic Church has joined in the debate about globalization and a new world order through the social encyclical of Pope Benedict XVI, *Caritas in Veritate*. The encyclical is dedicated to the memory and new reception of *Populorum Progressio*, the encyclical by Pope Paul VI on integral human development published more than 40 years ago. Among the changes that have taken place since then the encyclical raises up the "explosion of worldwide interdependence," that is, globalization (no. 33). Globalization is a priori neither good nor bad. It offers opportunities and carries risks. The financial and economic crisis of the early 21st century means that the process of economic globalization urgently needs to be placed under clear political direction and supervision (no. 41/2). In this context, the encyclical calls for the creation of a "true world political authority" vested with effective power "to ensure security for all, regard for justice, and respect for rights" (no. 67).[6]

This study is an attempt to deal with the experiences and challenges gained through the many years of my work at the World Council of Churches, most recently as general secretary from 1993 to 2003. As a fellowship that now counts about 350 member churches from all regions of the world, the WCC is the biggest and one of the oldest nongovernmental organizations with consultative status at the United Nations. The role of the public political responsibility that churches share for justice and peace in a new world order has shaped the work of the WCC since its founding in 1948. The intense and controversial debates over worldwide economic and social development, the realization of human rights and the struggle against racism, over nuclear weapons and disarmament, climate change and the preservation of creation, and the continuing search in all of these issues for the foundations and criteria for a political ethic in a global context are among my most important experiences in my three-decade-plus involvement with the WCC.

The historic political upheaval of 1989–1990 that brought with it the end of the confrontation between the Eastern and Western blocs and the rapid spread of the process of globalization obliges us to rethink many of the convictions that existed until then about a future world order. The first Gulf War of 1991, the armed conflicts in the former Yugoslavia from 1992 to 1999, the genocide in Rwanda in 1994, as well as the numerous "new wars" in the Caucasus, Sudan, and West Africa, in the Philippines, and in Indonesia have led to intense debates about nonmilitary, political forms of conflict resolution, and responsibility for the protection of populations that are victims of the military use of force. Such debates have become more intense through the spread of international terrorism. Apart from this, the WCC has participated intensively in the major world conferences of the United Nations on environment and development (Rio 1992), human rights (Vienna 1993), social development (Copenhagen 1995), the role and the rights of women (Beijing 1995), racism (Durban 2001), and in the respective follow-up conferences. Through these conferences and through the controversial debate about the consequences of economic and financial globalization, the WCC has been increasingly pulled into to the search for a sustainable world order.[7]

One of the particular challenges was and is linked to the entry of the major world religions into the global public space. The Parliament of the World's Religions gave a clear signpost with its "Declaration Toward a Global Ethic" in Chicago noted above. The WCC has for many years played a consultative role in the initiatives of the World Conference of Religions for Peace. As WCC general secretary I was invited to events with "religious and spiritual leaders" at the Millennium World Peace Summit (2000), a meeting of the World Economic Forum (2002), a consultation of the International Labour Office about the "Philosophical and Spiritual Dimensions on Decent Work" (2002), a meeting of the InterAction Council (2003), and of the Europe Economic Forum (2006). It became clear to me as I took part in these events that there was a need for a more fundamental evaluation of the relationship between religion and politics and of the way in which they exercise their responsibility for social order in both the national and international context. The expectations that economic leaders and politicians have of religions and their leaders as guardians of the moral and ethical traditions of humanity, and of their ability to mediate in the current situations of conflict, requires religions, and not least Christian churches, to engage in critical self-reflection about their action in the public space.

After leaving the WCC I had the opportunity to deal in greater detail with these issues both theoretically and practically, as the only representative of a religious organization to be appointed to the "Helsinki Process on Globalization and Democracy." Within this process, which concluded in 2008, I had many opportunities to deepen my reflections on issues of religion and politics and to test them with experts from all areas of public life. Two teaching assignments—at Harvard Divinity School (2005/6) and the Ecumenical Institute Bossey (2006/7)—offered the possibility through seminars with students to go more deeply into the ethical issues linked to the relationship of power, law, and morality, as well as the different entry points of religious traditions into the relationship between religion and politics.

What I now present in this study are the preliminary conclusions of a path of discovery that has certainly not come to an end. In the course of my reflections I have found that the issues of religion and politics are the subject of lively academic debate, especially in the Anglo-Saxon world, which has resulted in numerous publications. The chapters that follow testify my debt to such investigations, although the choice of the research from the political, social, and religious sciences is to a certain extent arbitrary and makes no claims to academic completeness. I am aware that in this study I am dealing with an area that lies outside my own academic competence. I have therefore abstained from engaging in critical debate with the various positions and research that are presented here. My interest is not to join in a discussion among established experts but, rather, to consider and to critically reflect upon the various experiences that have been mentioned and the challenges that become apparent in a wider context.

My roots in the ecumenical movement of the Christian churches and my longstanding interest in the issues of Christian political ethics and the responsibility of churches in the public political space is, of course, able to be discerned in the chapters that follow. However, I have concentrated on the issues that affect all religions, naturally including Christianity.

In working on this study, I have received suggestions, encouragement, and constructive criticism from my longstanding colleagues and friends Martin Robra (Geneva), Heinrich Schäfer (Bielefeld), and Wolfram Stierle (Berlin). The continual exchange with my wife, Elisabeth, and the discussion with my four sons, Martin, Ulrich, Simon, and Christoph, all of whom have their own expertise in many of the issues discussed here, was and continues to be of particular importance to me. This book is dedicated to them.

1. Religion and Politics in Conflict?

THE RETURN OF RELIGION TO THE PUBLIC SPHERE

One of the most striking features of the world's current upheavals is that politicians and business leaders repeatedly look to humanity's religious traditions in the hope that a dialogue of cultures and religions might help create a culture of mutual responsibility among citizens and communities, thereby engendering a solid foundation for efforts to create a new world order.[1] There are, however, strong reasons to be somewhat skeptical as to whether religions are able to make such a contribution toward shaping a new, sustainable world order. We have seen only too clearly the many conflicts of recent times in which the protagonists legitimized their policies through the use of religious values or by stirring up religious passions and loyalties. Even if it is conceded that most of these conflicts are due not to religious differences but have political or economic origins, religious traditions nevertheless seem to possess a potential for violence that can be used at will to advance sectional interests and objectives.

It is the so-called monotheistic religions of Judaism, Christianity, and Islam that are the principal targets of this critique. Some scholars say, for example, that their zeal to enforce the truth of the one God is evidence of their "inherent violence."[2] While they concede that these religions have taken crucial steps toward overcoming traditional hierarchies and boundaries between nations and ethnic groups, races and classes, establishing a powerful religious universalism through the principle of the equality of all believers, they assert that this has been at the cost of making a radical distinction between believers and unbelievers:

> The seed of religiously motivated violence lies in the universalism of the equality of believers which withholds from non-believers what it promises to believers: dignity for fellow human beings and equality in a world of strangers. […] Whoever declares him- or herself in favour of belief will be saved. Whoever neither will nor can believe will be damned—in this world and the next. The distinction between 'we' and the 'others' becomes emotionally charged by the cosmic struggle between the 'powers of good' that have to overcome the 'powers of evil' if the world is to be saved. In this way, the absolute nature of the one-and-only monotheistic God creates an entire world of 'others' who have to be combated.[3]

These provocative claims are based on an idiosyncratic interpretation of the source material, especially the biblical texts. In his book about the alleged dangers of religion,[4] the Berlin theologian Rolf Schieder has convincingly refuted such claims. The "monotheism theory," however, is just one of the apparent threats for which religions are held responsible. Many people find the religiously motivated terrorism emanating from fundamentalist movements still more threatening. In his book *Terror in the Mind of God*, published even before the attacks of September 2001, the American sociologist Mark Juergensmeyer studies the global increase in religiously motivated violence, examining five case studies in the United States, Israel, Palestine, India, and Japan.[5] He concludes that those who commit such acts are making symbolic statements. Their political strategy is to use religious images and the symbols of a cosmic war between the children of light and the children of darkness to create a climate of fear and a readiness to engage in an all-embracing spiritual conflict that demands an "all-or-nothing" response, and in which no compromise is possible. Juergensmeyer points out that symbolic representations of violence can be found in all religions: violence is sacralized by a "spiritual battle," since only thus can the violent experiences of chaos, death, disorder, destruction, and decay be brought under control. At the same time, this symbolic legitimization of violence often compensates for experiences of powerlessness and humiliation. This is particularly the case for young men in the Islamic world, for whom social and professional marginalization is linked to their disillusionment with the model of society provided by secular nationalism and who are searching for an alternative based on religion.[6]

Religiously motivated terrorism is, of course, only the most dramatic, and in its influence probably overestimated, manifestation of a development that began in the 1970s and that has resulted in religions and religious movements becoming key actors on the political stage in many different contexts. Until a few decades ago, the dominant and barely questioned belief was that the influence of religion on the organization of social and political life would decline and that religions would be relegated to the private sphere of purely personal views. Religious beliefs should thus, it was argued, be kept out of the rational business of politics and business. This was expressed in demands for a clear separation between religion and politics, so as to keep the organization of the political order free from the influence of religious principles.

This tacit assumption has been challenged in recent times by the emergence of religious movements with overtly political aspirations. There have already been several studies of such developments. Thus, in his book first published in 1991, *The Revenge of God: Resurgence of Islam, Christianity and Judaism in the Modern World*, Gilles Kepel, a French sociologist and researcher of Islam, studies conservative and fundamentalist movements such as the Muslim Brotherhood in Egypt and the Islamic revolution in Iran, the Catholic movement "Communion and Liberation" (*Communione e Liberazione*), the New Christian Right in the United States, and the Gush Emunim ("Block of the Faithful") movement in Israel. All of these movements, he concludes, radically call into question the fundamentals of secular modernity, and thus also the separation of religion and politics, and seek a fundamental reorganization of the world based on religious principles.[7]

Other studies have placed these developments in a broader global context, interpreting the growing public influence of religious movements and organizations as evidence for the need to revise the conventional idea that modernization leads to the progressive secularization, that is, privatization, of religion. Thus Jeff Haynes in his 1998 book *Religion in Global Politics* examines the processes of "deprivatization" of religion in different regions of the world. His conclusion is that religions gain new influence in the public sphere when they contribute to the defense of the endangered cultural identity of a social group, strengthening its internal solidarity in a situation of cultural change. "In sum," Haynes states, "the key to understanding the contemporary socio-political role of religion is that it regularly furnishes the resources for groups to try to deal with the effects stemming either from the processes of modernization or the contradictions of post-modernity."[8]

Meanwhile, Juergensmeyer has produced a revised and updated version of his earlier study, *The New Cold War? Religious Nationalism Confronts the Secular State* (1992). In his 2008 book, *Global Rebellion: Religious Challenges to the Secular State, from Christian Militias to al Qaeda*, Juergensmeyer argues that "the revival of religious politics at the dawn of the twenty-first century is due in large part to the loss of faith in secular nationalism in an increasingly globalized world."[9] In the course of decolonization and the beginnings of modernization in former colonial states, secular nationalism became the dominant ideology of state building. Leaders of religious and cultural minorities, in particular, as well as members of the educated, urban elites, willingly adopted the "spirit of secular nationalism." Nationalism took the place formerly occupied by religion as the glue that held society together. This development, influenced as it was by the European Enlightenment, now faces increasingly strident opposition, especially in the regions of the southern hemisphere, where the social and political order is still anchored in practices and customs shaped by religious traditions. In these countries we are therefore dealing with two competing frameworks of social order: secular nationalism (allied with the nation-state) and religion (allied with large ethnic communities, in part transnational):[10]

> Because religion ... and secular nationalism are ideologies of order, they are potential rivals. Either can claim to be the guarantor of orderliness within a society; either can claim to be the ultimate authority for social order. Such claims carry with them an extraordinary degree of power, for contained within them is the right to give moral sanction for life-and-death decisions, including the right to kill. When either secular nationalism or religion assumes that role by itself, it reduces the other to a peripheral social role.[11]

As ideologies of social order, religion and secular nationalism have such a close structural and functional equivalent, according to Juergensmeyer, that the dividing line between them has always been quite thin: "Both are expressions of faith, both involve an identity with and a loyalty to a large community, and both insist on the ultimate moral legitimacy of the authority invested in the leadership of that community."[12] In its cultural expression secular nationalism shows itself to be a "Western construct" and is therefore considered by many in the global South as a "mask for a certain form of European Christian culture" that needs to be resisted.[13] Particularly for those who had welcomed secular nationalism with almost messianic expectations, disappointment at the failure of its blessings to materialize is turned into its "satanization."[14] This results in different forms of religious politics based on a hazardous attempt to combine religion and the modern ideologies of nationalism and transnationalism. In his book, Juergensmeyer analyzes the manifestations of this "religious rebellion" against secular nationalism, starting with its origins in the Middle East, via the regions of Asia to Eastern Europe and the United States. A separate chapter is devoted to the transnationalization of the rebellion in the form of "global jihad."

In a comprehensive analysis of the role of religion in the context of globalization, Peter Beyer concludes that while the instrumental rationality of social systems and economic policies inexorably drives religion into the private sphere, new religious movements are developing and operating in the public, political sphere. Such movements are a reaction to the contradiction between the officially proclaimed values of the global system such as equality and progress, and its actual consequences as seen in increasing structural inequality and marginalization.[15] Like all social movements, they have their place in the lifeworld that determines the collective identity of social groups, and they mediate traditional religious functions and new social challenges in the context of globalization. Beyer examines five case studies: the new Christian Right in the United States, movements of liberation theology in Latin America, the Islamic revolution in Iran, the new religious Zionism in Israel, and the ecumenically inspired environmental movement. Despite their obvious differences, all these movements have two main similarities: (1) they mobilize around the unresolved problems of the global system and thus behave in an "antisystemic" fashion; and (2) they address these problems by attempting to influence the dominant social systems, especially the political and legal systems. This may take the form of the defense of religious and cultural identities against the relativizing forces of globalization, and be linked to nationalist aspirations. The movements may also, as in the case of liberation theology or comparable ecumenical endeavours, direct themselves to the creation of a new global culture of solidarity and thus the transformation of the global system itself. This confirms the observation that the "return" of religion in the public sphere is, at least indirectly, a consequence of the process of globalization. A critical examination of the traditional notions of the relationship between religion and politics is required, to the extent that the state-centred model of the political order has reached its limits as a result of globalization.

Religion and Politics: What Are We Talking About?

Up until now we have been employing the words *religion* and *politics* in very general terms without defining how they are being used. Such clarification is particularly necessary given that the apparent changes in the relationship between religion and politics, and the critical discussion about the alleged "return" of religion to the public sphere, is at least partly related to different approaches in dealing with the social reality of religion and politics. Each attempt at a definition raises more questions than it can answer. Despite this, we need to clarify the terms we are talking about to arrive at a working definition.

In the case of "religion," any definition depends on whether it is based on a functional or a substantive understanding of religion. The functional definition of religion, first developed by Emile Durkheim within the sociology of religion and still very influential, sees religion as a system of beliefs and practices that promotes the social integration of a social group.[16] The substantive definition of religion goes back to the early attempts to elaborate a phenomenological understanding of religion and sees the relationship to transcendence as being central to all forms of religion. Such a definition may be based on religious symbolic systems and the ideas they express about the general order of existence, or it may relate to religious experience and religious practice as ways of dealing with contingency in human life. Any such definition has its justification and its plausibility in the context of a reference system of given theoretical assumptions. This relativity of all definitions applies particularly to the commonly accepted understanding of religion in the European tradition, which is focused on an organized system of religious teachings and on the form of institutionalized religious bodies. This understanding of religion, based on the historical forms of Christianity and the related distinction between religion and culture, cannot simply be applied to other social and cultural contexts: "In cultures where religion is an integral part of the whole of life and is not separated out as a separate area, where it is understood as a path for the whole of the life of the community and of the individuals within it, as in Eastern cultures, or as the basis of all forms of life, as in tribal societies ... then a specific concept that refers only to religion is largely absent."[17]

In the context of this study that focuses on the relationship of religion and politics, the definitional discussions in the science and philosophy of religion can complement each other. At any rate there is a growing trend to do away with a "definition" of religion, and instead to concentrate on the description and analysis of religious practice.[18] This would mean taking into account both the subjective and objective aspects of religious practice, that is to say, the perspective of individual religiosity and its collective expressions, as well as its emotional and cognitive dimensions.

The *Religion Monitor 2008* published by the Bertelsmann Stiftung uses a grid of six *core dimensions* of religiosity that come from the sociology of religion, that is, "intellect, ideology (belief), public practice, private practice, experience, consequences."[19] In the context of this study, Martin Riesebrodt has produced a helpful analysis in stating that religious practice rests on three basic assumptions that distinguish it from other forms of social action, namely: (1) the assumed existence of "supernatural" personal or impersonal powers whose actions (2) control dimensions of human social life that normal social actors cannot control directly by their own power, and to which there is nevertheless (3) access by certain forms of practice or communication. Religious practice is thus directed at those dimensions of human life that are beyond the routine technical control of a given society and for the management of which the intervention of supernatural powers appears necessary. Religious institutions can thus be understood as the ensemble of rules and norms that regulate the interaction between human and superhuman powers.[20] Religious practice and religious institutions have therefore to do with power, or, as Rolf Schieder puts it: "Religion is the management of power."[21] Thus religion inevitably finds itself in tension with other manifestations of power and authority, especially when it comes to preventing and resolving crises.

Religious practice is different from other forms of social practice through its reference to transcendence, in making a fundamental distinction between immanence and transcendence, although transcendence does not necessarily need to be interpreted in terms of a conception of God. Instead, it expresses that religion in its symbolic practice is directed toward the meaning of reality as a whole.[22] According to Detlef Pollack, the problem of contingency and the meaning of all existence is at the very centre of religion:

> By introducing the distinction between immanence and transcendence, religion narrows the horizons of the world and converts the indeterminate of the world into the determinate. In this way it makes contingency bearable. . . . The issue for religion is thus, that if it wants to deal with contingencies, it needs to make the transcendent accessible. . . . Only if both things can be guaranteed—the reference to transcendence and its accessibility in the immanent—are religious forms able to fulfil their function of dealing with contingency.[23]

For the purpose of a working definition, the proposal of Theo Sundermeier may suffice, who "defined" religion as follows: "Religion is the communal response of a human being to the experience of transcendence, which is expressed in ritual and ethics."[24] Within this understanding of religion Sundermeier distinguishes between "primary and secondary religious experience," thereby expressing that the phenomena of coping with the world and the experience of religion are interdependent. The limited experience of reality of self-contained small groups or tribal societies corresponds to "primary religion." Such "primary religions" express experiences that contain a universal claim to validity. They influence and shape their societies, ethics, and culture through symbols and rituals. These primary experiences are clearly present within all religions. The "secondary religious experience" comes into play when there is a change in the perception of reality: "To the extent that the smaller society is destroyed or is called into question . . . and changes to become a larger society, so there needs to be a new way of coping with the world. The traditional conception no longer applies. In the religious sphere, this process of change is sensed, predicted, initiated and managed by seers, prophets and reformers. The larger society leaves people to their own devices in a broader space of decision making and choice."[25] "Secondary religion" is thus characterized by increasing individualization. It takes on conceptual rationality, thereby becoming a system able to be transmitted and characterized by a claim to universality.

The analytical distinction between primary and secondary religion should not, however, be understood as signifying a historical development from "primitive" to "high religion," since secondary religious experience does not simply replace primary religion but, rather, presupposes it: "The primary religious experience is the foundation on which the secondary is superimposed."[26] Sundermeier holds that "every world religion is based on the synthesis of two experiences, and is conditioned by the living, unfinished process of these two experiences."[27] From a historical and philosophical perspective, the fundamental change from the "primary" to "secondary" religion may be interpreted with the help of the theory of the "Axial Age," as Karl Jaspers characterized the intellectual and religious upheavals in the period from 800 to 200 BCE.[28]

Defining what is meant by "politics" faces similar problems to those encountered in defining religion. A look at current scholarly encyclopedias and reference books shows that there is no consensus as to how politics is to be understood. Each definition is based on different historical, cultural, and ideological assumptions. In the European tradition, politics is primarily associated with the state and state action. In his famous lecture of 1919, "Politics as a Vocation," Max Weber responds to the question, "What do we understand by politics?": "The concept is extremely broad and comprises any kind of *independent* leadership in action." He continues: "We wish to understand by politics only the leadership, or the influencing of the leadership, of a *political* association, hence today, of a *state* . . . a state is a human community that (successfully) claims the *monopoly of the legitimate use of physical force* within a given territory." And a little later, he states: "Hence, 'politics' for us means striving to share power or striving to influence the distribution of power, either among states or among groups within a state. . . . He who is active in politics strives for power either as a means in serving other aims, ideal or egoistic, or as 'power for power's sake,' that is, in order to enjoy the prestige-feeling that power gives."[29]

By tying politics to the state and the pursuit of power, Max Weber is part of the tradition of European modernity that goes back to Niccolo Machiavelli and Thomas Hobbes, which disengaged itself from the older tradition of understanding of politics developed by Plato and Aristotle in Greek philosophy. In this latter understanding, politics is related to the *polis* as the basic form of communal life, as Hannah Arendt has underlined in her writings.[30] *Politeia* refers to the space for the life of an ordered community, and particularly the participation of free citizens in shaping this order, which is directed to a "good life in righteousness." Politics in this sense as an expression of concern for "public affairs" was clearly defined and distinguished by Aristotle from the *Oeconomica*, which he saw as a matter for the "private" household, understood as *oikos* and thus needing to be kept apart from the "public space" of the *politeia*. In this tradition, particularly in that founded by Aristotle and which continued in the Roman philosophy of the state, politics was an integral part of practical, that is, ethical, philosophy.

This tradition persisted in the thought of Augustine and Thomas Aquinas, and still influenced how politics was understood in the European Middle Ages. A fundamental change began with the Renaissance and the beginnings of modernity. This break with the classical conception of politics is expressed most clearly in the thought of Machiavelli,[31] which quite intentionally severed the traditional connection between politics and ethics (or religion). Politics was "secularized" and reorganized as the theory and practice of acquiring and exercising power, applied to the state as the ruling apparatus. *Raison d'etat* replaced the former ethical rationale for politics. The Wars of Religion and the rise of absolutism, together with the revolutionary movements of the 18th and 19th centuries, strengthened and consolidated this secular understanding of politics, liberated from moral and religious control.

Compared to this étatist understanding, the Anglo-Saxon tradition, and particularly the American tradition influenced by Puritanism, has preserved an older understanding of politics and its ethical justification. Politics as the practice of governance, that is, the leadership of a community, is understood here as a function of society and is linked to the recognition of the legal system (common law). The self-organization of society, including the religious dimension, takes precedence over politics. To a large extent, this tradition lacks a counterpart to the European conception of the state. Politics refers to those specific actions that are characteristic for the task of leadership, that is, the tactics and strategy used in the political process.

The differences between these two traditions have narrowed since the Second World War, mainly due to the fact that democracy has become an accepted constitutional form while the economy has simultaneously emerged as an autonomous power centre. The role of the state vis-à-vis society has thus changed, and politics is no longer solely related to the state and the struggle for power. The field of politics is not confined to the institutional political system, that is, the government, administration, parliament, political parties, courts, and their formal decision-making authority. As Erhard Eppler puts it, "Politics has always had to do with how people live and how, mostly very decidedly, they do not want to live. Civil society is the most primordial instrument available, which people use so that they can live the way they want to live.... To that extent, civil society is a place of politics."[32]

In contrast to the prevailing tendency in both traditions to focus on politics as the practice of governance and the means that are necessary for this, the issue of the objectives of politics—the question of the "good" or "sustainable" organization of the community—is now taking on a new significance. Alongside the guiding values of peace, justice, and human rights, the question of legitimacy is coming to the fore. In this expanded understanding, politics relates to all intentional actions in the public space. This "working definition" will be used and developed in the chapters that follow. Politics thus includes both the institutional *political system* (government), as well as the broader framework of *political society* as a complex of actions and initiatives that aim to influence institutional policies, and finally the *civil society*—the ensemble of all social groups, including religious communities, that take part in influencing public opinion and in determining the goals of political action.[33]

Religion and Politics in Premodern Societies

We turn now to the central question, namely the relationship and reciprocal influence between religion and politics in the shaping of the social order. The discussion so far has made clear that both religion and politics have to do with power and that both are constitutively related to the order of human society. Both religion and politics have to do with the integrity of human coexistence in community—although from different perspectives—and therefore with the issue of "the management of power" (Rolf Schieder). Even a very general description such as this suggests that religion and politics are in tension, because each of them has to do, albeit in different ways, with "the whole" of the life of human society and the way it is organized.

This underlying competitive relationship between religion and politics has, throughout history, led to different policies intended to prevent or at least to limit potential conflicts. It is possible to conceive three different "ideal types" of relationship: (1) religion recognized as the fundamental source of power and authority and thus the measure of the legitimacy of all forms and structures of governance (theocratic tendency); (2) politics exercising an absolute claim to power, including the control of religion up to and including the complete integration of religion into the state system

(Caesaro-papist tendency); (3) mutual distance, whether in the form of a clear institutional and legal separation of the spheres of religion and politics, with the secularization of politics and the privatization of religion (secular trend), or a conscious withdrawal of religion from public space into an inner world (ascetic/mystical/pietistic tendency). Making a distinction between these three "trends" helps us to analyze the complex relationship between religion and politics. In the way they have developed in history and in social reality, these trends have often been superimposed on each other, because both religion and politics represent fundamental dimensions of the life of the human community as their common field of reference.

We can say that in all premodern, traditional societies the specific roles and functions of religion and politics are scarcely differentiated. Such differentiation takes shape only over a longer period of time. What Sundermeier has identified as being characteristic of "smaller societies" and their primary religious experience also extends beyond tribal societies: an all-encompassing ordering of the world is expressed through symbolic forms, rituals, and rules of conduct. Maintaining this order and restoring it after ruptures is simultaneously a "political" and a "religious" task, and forms the core of the "culture" in question. The categories and distinctions traditionally used in rational analysis cannot simply be applied in a clear-cut fashion. The same goes for the distinction between the specific roles of priests, rulers, and judges. The order that is symbolically represented and ritually secured is simultaneously the source of law and legitimate governance.

To the extent to which self-contained and closed small societies become differentiated and transformed into larger units, so the experience of the world changes, as well as the way in which this order that supports this extended world is conceived. The mastery of the world (*Weltbewältigung*) that is now required leads to changes at the level of fundamental symbolization and ritual performance. Sundermeier interprets this transition in terms of the emergence of "secondary religions" that, together with a new value being placed on individuality, and a transcendentally founded order of existence aiming at universality, singles out "religion" as an independent dimension of life in society. Important elements of "primary religion" remain alive in all cultures, however, in the form of "popular religiosity." This changed experience of the world has implications for the processes of shaping and securing the social order. The area of "politics" in the form of continuous, institutional, and legal arrangements and the appointment of persons with extensive responsibility for leadership takes on a profile of its own, whether through the formation of city-states or feudally ordered empires. Nevertheless, "religion" and "politics" still remain inextricably related to each other in shared responsibility for "the whole" of the life of the community, and continue to be so related for a long period. "Politics" exercises its specific task within the framework of a religiously sanctioned order, from which all forms of governance or exercise of power receive their legitimacy.

Crucial for the differentiated and simultaneously charged relationship between religion and politics is the emergence of a legal system that extends beyond the control of ritual and cultic functions, and that maintains internal peace by placing the relationships of members of the community on a secure basis. All legal systems have their origin in sacred law, which reflects the transcendent order, and from thence receive their binding force. It was a priestly role, assigned to the area of religion, to ensure its respect and enforcement. Sacred law provided the framework within which the "political" governors, that is, judges and kings, could exercise their responsibilities for applying and making laws. The sacred foundations of the traditional fabric of law, morality, and ethics continued for a long time. It is not possible here to discuss the details of the complex historical development, particularly in Egypt, in the ancient Near East, and in the biblical-Israelite context that have been the subject of academic debate in recent years.[34] The contemporary discussion about how law and morality are distinct from or related to each other refers back to the original function of law as an intermediary between religion and politics.[35]

Within the general framework that could only be sketched out here, specific traditions regarding the correlation or differentiation of religion and politics have emerged in different cultural environments. A detailed description and analysis cannot be undertaken here and is not necessary for the limited purposes of this study. Despite criticism of certain details, Max Weber's research on the typology of domination, as well as on communal and associative relationships, and in this context on the sociology of religion, particularly its relationship to the world, may serve as a starting point for further discussion.[36] Weber's studies on the legitimacy of social and political orders and the characteristic forms of power and domination are of critical importance here. These correspond, as far as religious traditions are concerned, to differing symbolizations of transcendent reality (monotheistic, polytheistic, or pantheistic) and their relationship to and influence on the "world." The formation of wider social and political power structures is associated with the process of hierarchical structuring and the concentration of transcendent agencies.[37]

However one might interpret the apparent phenomenological differences, it was the emergence and political reception of monotheism in Israel and then in Christianity and Islam that led to the tension between religion and politics characteristic of the developments that followed. We have already mentioned the questionable and controversial interpretation of the available source material, especially the biblical narratives of Moses and the covenant at Sinai (Exodus 34), and the possible links to Egyptian traditions from the time of Pharaoh Akhenaten.[38] Despite some differences, especially over dating, research leaves little room for doubt that the worship of the one God, who makes a covenant with Israel as God's people, and at the same time is revealed as the creator and lord of the whole world, is the result of the critical appropriation of the failure of the political ambitions of the kingdoms of Israel and Judah in their disputes with the neighbouring Assyrian and Babylonian empires. There is no direct model for this in the ancient Near Eastern world.

The one God reveals the divine self through God's law, which determines the order of life of the people and to which the holders of political power are subjected. Through the recognition of the one God as the source of power, of law and of justice, a "secularization" of all traditional forms of "cosmic religiosity" is taking place. The cosmos as God's creation no longer serves as a religious symbol. The critique of the prophets who have a mandate from God to challenge royal power is the precursor to the fundamental critical distinction between religion and politics, which remains a leaven in the development of both Christianity and Islam.

We will deal in a later chapter with the particular way in which the idea of the unity of God and its consequences contributed to Islam's understanding of the relationship between religion and politics. To conclude this survey, we shall briefly review the emergence in Christianity of the way in which the relationship between religion and politics was conceived until the beginnings of modernity. In the first centuries CE, the Christian community remained clearly within the prophetic tradition of Jesus, whose proclamation of the rule of God that had dawned fundamentally challenged the religiously legitimized claims to power of the Roman emperor and the *Pax Romana* proclaimed by the emperor.[39] As followers of their Lord, who was himself a victim of Roman rule, the Christian community lived as a persecuted minority. Their witness to the reign and justice of the one God, and their example of how in their own lives they dealt with persecution, gradually gained acceptance until the so-called shift in the 4th century under Emperor Constantine, who—whether from conviction or from political expediency to preserve the unity and internal peace of the kingdom—recognized the Christian church as a legitimate religion (Edict of Tolerance, 313). Under Constantine's successor Theodosius I the persecuted minority became the official state religion. The one God of the Christian faith was now identified with the *deus summus,* the Roman state ideology. In his study of the emergence of the Byzantine state, Hendrik Berkhof arrives at the conclusion:

A state church and an Orthodox imperial ideology as a civic duty—this structure resembles the relationship of state and religion in the heathen Roman Empire like one drop of water resembles another.... In the deeper sense, the Christian church was not the victor in 313 but the loser, as it took the place of the old state religion and had to take on the character of this religion against its will and without any gratitude. It became a function of the life of the state and its faith degenerated to an external compulsory cultic act.[40]

In the years that followed, two different lines of tradition developed in the East and West of the imperial church. In the Byzantine tradition of the East, with its mystical and speculative emphasis on all-encompassing unity, the emperor was regarded as the earthly representative of the universal rule of God. He was responsible not only for maintaining peace and order in the kingdom, but also for protecting the true faith, including the persecution of dissenters and heretics. The relationship between religion and politics, and between church and state, was interpreted as a "symphony," that is, a close relationship of mutual responsibility and support. The relationship between state and church has often been interpreted as analogous to the relationship between body and soul. Each of the two sides was required to respect the specific role of the other, but together both were responsible for the unity of the empire as a hallowed space.

Unlike the Byzantinism that prevailed in the East with its tendency toward "Caesaropapism" and the high degree of passivity of the church hierarchy vis-à-vis the emperor, a genuinely theocratic tendency, reaffirming the prophetic tradition, developed in the West, influenced by Ambrose and his active commitment to the freedom of the church. According to this perspective, the emperor is a son of the church and does not stand over her, so he has no right to intervene in the life of the church. Even in nonecclesiastical matters, the emperor is to obey the commandment of God, and the church has the prophetic task, *in extremis*, to call the emperor to obedience to God's word if he deviates from it in his actions. This primacy of the freedom of the church continued in the West until the Middle Ages. Berkhof notes: "There is a direct line from Milan (the dispute between Ambrose and the Arian Emperor Valentine II) to Canossa (the submission of Henry IV in the Investiture Controversy); it denotes the unity of church and state in the sense that even the holder of the highest state power, because he is a Christian, is subject to the moral commandments of the church and thus the instrument according to God's will for the construction of a Christian social order."[41] We do not need to deal here with further developments in the West from Augustine, via Gelasius, to Pope Gregory VII. To the extent, however, that the theocratic tendency solidified the belief that the emperor's authority ultimately derives from the church, an ethical and theological principle became an issue of power. Berkhof concludes: "If the church identifies its own authority with the authority of the Word with which it has been entrusted, and sees its obedience to this authority being fulfilled in its obedience to the Pope, it has silently mistaken God's business for its own business. It was to this distortion that the theocratic idea fell victim in the Middle Ages."[42]

Redefining the Relationship between Religion and Politics in Modern Europe

The two traditions briefly described here remained in place until the beginnings of modernity and even beyond. The Eastern tradition of the symphony between church and state and the legitimacy it received through the theology of the Byzantine Empire remained determinative in Eastern Europe with its Greek and Slavic influence. After the conquest of Constantinople in 1453 and the end of the Eastern Roman Empire this tradition continued in the national Orthodox churches of the East, especially in Russia, with the claim of Moscow as the "third (and last) Rome" taking the place of the

Byzantine Empire. Even the later Ottoman Empire saw itself as the "regulatory political successor" of Byzantium.[43]

In the West, however, developments until the end of the Thirty Years' War were determined by the conflict between *sacerdotium* and *imperium*, between the papacy and the newly established "Holy Roman Empire of German Nation." The struggle for the freedom of the church from the religiously legitimated power of the empire reached an initial culmination with the *dictatus papae* of Pope Gregory VII in 1075. But the "papal revolution"[44] and the universal claim to power of the papacy that it entailed led only to a new phase of the conflict, ultimately acting as a catalyst for the increasing emancipation of politics from a unitary culture founded upon religion. This process of emancipation began in the Italian city-states that were the first to develop a purely secular political structure. It found its theoretical expression in the writings of Niccolo Machiavelli (1469–1527), whose understanding of politics was the "sum of resources that are necessary to acquire power, to maintain power and to make best use of power, whether to win friends, weaken enemies or to widen one's own sphere of influence."[45] According to Machiavelli, the state is a secular order and religion is to be judged by whether or not it is useful to the state. He rejected the autonomous authority of religion and the order that it proclaims; this is the basis for his opposition to Christianity as embodied by the Roman church of his time. *Raison d'etat* takes the place of the religious legitimization of measures to maintain the state order.

The most momentous opposition to the unity of the *corpus christianum* characterized by the conflict-ridden interplay between emperor and pope came with the Protestant Reformation in northern Europe. Its political momentum was based on the early emancipation of the cities and principalities from imperial sovereignty, as well as the social revolution of the Peasants' War. The conflict was not only about the unity of the church, but also and especially about the unity of the empire, which was ultimately guaranteed through the unity of religion. Only when it was demonstrated that military means could not guarantee this unity was there a preliminary convergence in the Augsburg Religious Peace of 1555 on the basis of *"cuis regio eius religio"* ("whose realm, his religion") through the imperial recognition of the *Confessio Augustana*. This meant, in effect, the end of the political and religious unity of the empire. The traditional guiding principle of the *corpus christianum*, however, remained intact. "Because it could no longer be sustained in the imperial territory, it was returned to the level of the territories of the sovereign princes where there could still be only one faith. However, this led at the same time to a theologically consummated rupture with the ideal of the unity of Christendom, since the basis of *'cuis regio eius religio'* was determined precisely by the fact of confessional division."[46] The emergence of territorial states and of confessional territorial churches (*Kirchentümer*) has the same roots.

The agreement reached in the Augsburg Religious Peace was, however, of only limited duration. The political tensions that followed the Counter-Reformation reopened the conflict and expanded it to the European level. The question of whether it is appropriate to refer to the Thirty Years' War as a war of religions is still disputed in historical research. Without doubt, the confessionalization of Christendom that began in the second half of the 16th century created a situation where confessional identities could be used to mobilize the population in political conflicts. Religion served as a basis of legitimacy and as a way to stigmatize other believers as "heretics." In this climate, tolerance was seen as a betrayal of true religion.

The Peace of Westphalia, which ended the Thirty Years' War in 1648, is often viewed as the beginning of the process of the secularization of politics in Europe and as the basis of the system of sovereign nation-states. Recent studies indicate, however, that a close connection between religion and politics continued long after that date in the European tradition and if anything was reinforced during the era of absolutism. On the other hand, the passions invested in religious conflicts had largely been exhausted by the end of the 17th century, so that the secular political language available since Machiavelli and developed by Hugo Grotius and Thomas Hobbes was able to slowly gain acceptance. Therefore, even if the idea and rituals of a God-ordained rule of kings remained in existence for some time, there was a gradual development toward understanding politics and governance as a human institution with the task of guaranteeing the peace and welfare of citizens.[47]

Historical periodization sees the Peace of Westphalia as the end of the period of transition that began at the Renaissance, in which the closed world of the Middle Ages began to dissolve, and as the beginning of modernity. The Age of Enlightenment that subsequently began is characterized by the critical use of reason, the scientific study of nature, and the emancipation of the new bourgeoisie. Its underlying aim was the freedom of human beings, in the sense of responsibility and autonomy from all external authority, not least from religion.

Modernization and Secularization

With the French Revolution came the development that is now described by the term *secularization*. The initial measures undertaken by the National Assembly such as the confiscation of church property and the proclamation of the Civil Constitution of the Clergy, that is, the abolition of the clerical estate, were not fundamentally opposed to religion, but were mostly directed against the central power of the church in social and political life. In the course of the revolution, however, a radical, secular Enlightenment tendency prevailed. This led to a first step in 1795 toward separating church and state. In the conflict-ridden period that followed the Revolution these decisions were modified or partially withdrawn. It was only 100 years later that this fundamental decision was finally implemented through the 1905 law on the separation of church and state. The law prohibited state funding for the church(es) and banished religion from the public space. This secular orientation of the French constitutional tradition is still valid today, even if there are increasing demands for it to be revised, not least because of the presence of a large Muslim minority.

French secularism (*laïcité*) has been and is still seen as an expression of the religiously critical direction of the Enlightenment, whereas the Anglo-Saxon tradition of political enlightenment, based on Deism and ethics founded on natural law, maintained the idea of the interrelationship between religion and politics. This was expressed in the Declaration of Independence and the Constitution of the United States of America. The First Amendment (1791), which prohibits the establishment of a state church, as well as any restriction of the free exercise of religion, is also aimed at the separation of church and state. Unlike the French tradition, however, it was not intended to banish religion and the church from the public arena but, rather, to prevent any state or political interference in the sphere of religion. We will return to this difference in the next chapter.

The impetus of the French Revolution, and especially its anti-clerical orientation, spread to the neighbouring countries of continental Europe. Everything seemed to suggest that the traditional European system that had existed since the Peace of Westphalia of territorial churches with their close ties to the nation-states was coming to an end. Certainly, the churches took this development seriously, seeing it as a fundamental challenge. It seemed it would contest their hitherto largely unchallenged place in public life and their decisive influence on education, culture, and morals, and cut them off from the support they had hitherto received from the public authorities. It took almost a hundred years, however, until such tendencies prevailed.

These changes have been interpreted using the concept of "secularization." Originally this term referred to the transfer of church property rights to public authorities (the Principal Decree of the Imperial Deputation, 1803), analogous to the change in the status of priests or religious who left the clerical state and became "secularized." Since the beginning of the 20th century, however, the term has been used in a figurative sense to describe the impact of the social and cultural changes unleashed by industrialization and the spread of the modern scientific worldview on the self-understanding and the place of the churches in society. The confrontation with the process of secularization played a central role in European church and theological debates in the first half of the 20th century.

A theoretical version took the form of the theory of secularization as an inevitable consequence of the development of a modern, differentiated society as in the writings of Emile Durkheim and Max Weber. According to Durkheim, secularization designated a change in the social location and role of religion (not only of Christianity) as a consequence of the increasing functional differentiation of society. The division of labour leads to the economy, law, and education taking shape as distinct areas of society, each with its own rationality. Durkheim saw this differentiation of social functions and actors responsible for them as an inevitable consequence of the emergence of modern society. Whereas in the medieval system of the *corpus christianum* the church and the state authority together ensured the integration of these different functional areas, churches and religious communities became one functional actor among others, with the functions that are not religious in the strict sense being "secularized" and taken over by other actors. Durkheim himself was a staunch supporter of French *laïcité*.[48]

Max Weber followed a similar approach in his analysis, though he placed greater emphasis on the interpretation of the change in people's relationship to the world that began with the Enlightenment, and expressed in the increasing "rationalization" and "disenchantment" of the world. Science, technology, and instrumental reason take the place previously occupied by a religious or magical understanding of the world. The traditional role of religion, namely presenting an all-encompassing view of the world, is transferred to modern science. In his lecture, "Science as a Vocation," Weber warns against expecting that science will provide a binding interpretation of meaning as a sort of religious prophecy. To the person who cannot bear "like a man" the "fate of the times" in the shape of increasing rationalization, intellectualization, and the disenchantment of the world, "one must say: may he rather return . . . simply and plainly. The arms of the old churches are opened widely and compassionately for him. After all, they do not make it hard for him. One way or another he has to bring his 'intellectual sacrifice'—that is inevitable."[49]

A self-contained theory of secularization was developed, building on the studies of Durkheim and Weber. Its starting point was that the process of modernization accompanied by the increasing rational differentiation of social functions would push religious communities out of public life to the sphere of private life. As a result, religions would concentrate on the specifically religious functions of interpreting reality (*Sinndeutung*) and dealing with contingency through cultic and ritual exercises. While this might allow a space to develop to shape religious life that is independent of the state, without concern for the social order as a whole, the theory of secularization in its more radical, critical forms, and not only that of Marxism, was linked to an assumption that religions are increasingly marginal factors in the life of society, or even that they would simply die out.

The supporters of this theory, which became a central element in the formation of sociological theory, pointed to the manifest weakening of traditional church structures and the "de-ecclesiasticalization" (*Entkirchlichung*) of a broad strata of the population in European societies. The fact that the situation in the United States was clearly different was treated as an exception to this rule. There was also the expectation that, as a result of modernization and industrialization, other cultural and religious contexts, not influenced by the Christian tradition, would follow a similar process of secularization—that is, the diminishing influence of religion on public life.

This makes it all the more striking that an author such as Harvey Cox, whose book *The Secular City* caused a stir in the 1960s by praising secularism as an experience of liberation, would speak thirty years later about the "revival of religion" and the "return of the sacred."[50] Meanwhile, the sociologist Peter L. Berger, whose 1967 book *The Sacred Canopy* (also published under the title *The Social*

Reality of Religion) has long been considered a standard work of secularization theory, edited a volume in 2005 under the title *The Desecularization of the World*. In it he states: "My point is that the assumption that we live in a secularized world is false. The world today, with some exceptions ... is as furiously religious as it ever was, and in some places more so than ever. This means that a whole body of literature by historians and social scientists loosely labeled 'secularization theory' is essentially mistaken." Berger is here questioning the assumption that modernization "necessarily leads to a decline of religion, both in society and in the minds of individuals."[51]

CRITIQUE AND THE FURTHER DEVELOPMENT OF SECULARIZATION THEORY

Discussions in recent decades have shown that both the concept of secularization and the sociological theory that buttresses it, along with its reception, are ambiguous and require further clarification. It is thus a helpful development that several attempts have been made recently to formulate the theory more precisely and to differentiate its various dimensions and aspects more clearly. This is still more important if the theory is to stand up to critical empirical examination. In an analysis of the available literature published in 1981, the Belgian Catholic sociologist Karel Dobbelaere proposed distinguishing between "societal secularization" (corresponding to the Durkheimian concept of social differentiation), "organizational secularization" (i.e., the corresponding changes in religious organization), and "individual secularization" (referring to changes in individual religious behaviour and in the systems of religious belief, i.e., especially the relativity of absolute truth-claims).[52] It then becomes clear that there is no necessary connection between these three dimensions of secularization.

The research of the Spanish-American sociologist José Casanova in his book *Public Religions in the Modern World* is particularly helpful in this regard. He sees the core of secularization theory that is still valid in the thesis of the "process of functional differentiation and emancipation of the secular spheres—primarily the state, the economy, and science—from the religious sphere and the concomitant differentiation and specialization of religion within its own newly found religious sphere."[53] He distinguishes between this central thesis and two other subtheses that have been derived from it, namely the inevitable decline of religion and its privatization and marginalization in the modern world. It is these two subtheses whose credibility is called into question by the empirical data.

One consequence of the critical differentiation that is required is the need to concede that a general theory of secularization is no longer tenable. The concept and the theory are both of European origin and Casanova is correct to state in a later essay from 2003 that they need to be seen in their historical context:

> From a global historical perspective the series of changes we call secularization evince an internal dynamic unique to a particular form of religious regime, Western Christendom and its Catholic and Protestant derivatives, which has very few parallels in other world religions, or even in the oldest and most traditional forms of Christianity, the Eastern Churches. In order to facilitate genuine comparative historical analyses, we need to dissociate the historical theory of European secularization from general theories of modernization. The secularization of Europe is a particular, unique and 'exceptional' historical process, not a universal teleological model of development which shows the future to the rest of the world.[54]

As far as the process of modernization is concerned, there is increasing acceptance for Shmuel N. Eisenstadt's claim that modernization takes different forms according to the historical and cultural context.[55]

The same historical relativism is also called for when it comes to the general theory that religion will decline as a result of modernization. This theory has its origin in a particular form of Enlightenment thought that became linked to a general critique of religion, and which has been revived by various parties today. It became a political ideology in the rationalism of the French Revolution and Marxism. While the Enlightenment prepared the ground for the development of modern science, the idea of a fundamental opposition between science and religion remained largely confined, however, to Europe. Modern instrumental rationality has indeed banished religion to the "private" realm of subjectivity, but it is the paradox of this rational interpretation of the world that has led to the new question about religion in the public space.

The apparent vitality of religion in the global South and its incipient revival in postmodern societies, therefore, cannot be really described as an expression of "desecularization." Indeed, we need to give much greater attention to the contextual, historical, cultural, and sociopolitical factors than has hitherto been the case for much of the research. This is also the case for the concept of "postsecularism" introduced into the discussion by Jürgen Habermas. In his acceptance speech at the reception of the German Book Trade Peace Prize in 2001, Habermas spoke of the "postsecular society which adapts to the fact that religious communities continue to exist in a context of ongoing secularization."[56] With this concept Habermas bids farewell to his previous position of equating social modernization with the secularization of society. Instead, he advocates a process of learning that makes it possible to translate ongoing living religious beliefs into the categories of secular reason. In a later text, his speech for the reception of the Holberg Prize in 2005, Habermas explicitly addresses the increased presence of religion in the public sphere and calls for the widening of the liberal conception of democratic citizenship and the principle of separation of state and church, or of politics and religion, toward a recognition of the cognitive and moral heritage of religions that has still not been exhausted under modern, postmetaphysical conditions.[57] Nevertheless, the main point of reference remains the secular understanding of the democratic state and its public culture, including the separation of religion and politics. That this constitutive framework itself is due to a unique form of cultural and historical process with its origin in a particular expression of religion, that is, the Judeo-Christian tradition and its particular form in Western Christianity, is indirectly acknowledged,[58] but this insight does not lead to a truly self-critical relativization of secular consciousness. In the final analysis, even the concept of "postsecularism" remains trapped in the assumptions of secularization theory.

Nevertheless, this confirms that religion needs to continue to be taken seriously as a central dimension of human existence. While for a long time it was largely displaced in its various aspects from the public sphere, there is again a public awareness of religion. Admittedly, it is also clear that the special form of "public religion" as it has existed in the territorial churches in Europe analogous to states is hardly sustainable. These churches may be able to continue to function for a little while as a sort of "vicarious religion." Grace Davie, from whom this term stems, describes it as meaning that "significant numbers of Europeans are content to let both churches and churchgoers enact a memory on their behalf, . . . more than half aware that they might need to draw on the capital at crucial times in their individual or collective lives."[59] At the same time it is clear, and the Religion Monitor confirms this for Germany, that the process of increasing individualization of the search for meaning and certainty is probably irreversible and that the traditional Christian religious communities will be increasingly assimilated into civil society and thus will need to adapt to a situation of cultural and religious pluralism.

It remains to be seen whether the so-called New Religious Movements, formed on a Christian and/or syncretistic basis, responding to the individualization of religion and transforming it at the same time into new forms of communal relationships (*Vergemeinschaftung*), will bring forth their own form of "public religion." Some of the examples presented in the following chapter point in this direction. At any rate there are indications that religious communities and religious movements are trying to position themselves in the global competition for power and political influence. They are aware that these new forms of political involvement of "public religion" do not mean turning their back on the arduous, hard-fought secular separation of religion and politics. Instead, both religion and politics inevitably have to do with power and are in latent tension with one another. The clear delineation of functions and sectors, as it evolved as a result of the process of secularization, is only one of the historically determined processes of the underlying tension and cannot be generalized. Instead, under the pressure of the process of globalization, all religions are being forced to reflect in a new and critical way on the relationship between religion and politics.

2. Beyond Church and State

THE PUBLIC SPACE: STATE AND POLITICS

In the previous chapter, we referred to the analytical model that distinguishes, in the case of modern, democratic societies, between the state, political society, and civil society. All three areas taken together constitute the "public space" of a political community. The term *state* refers to the institutional political system, that is, government, administration, parliament, and judiciary. The *political society* represents the democratic process of influencing public opinion and decision making that is undertaken by political parties, trade unions, associations, media, and other groups that aim to influence institutional politics and its decisions. Finally, the core of *civil society* is made up of those "nongovernmental and noneconomic connections and voluntary associations that anchor the communication structures of the public sphere in the society component of the lifeworld. Civil society is composed of those more or less spontaneously emergent associations, organizations, and movements that, attuned to how societal problems resonate in the private life spheres, distil and transmit such reactions in amplified form to the public sphere."[1]

Behind this differentiated model of "public space" is a communicative understanding of the public sphere and a critical development of the traditional distinction between the "public" sphere and the "private" sphere. Picking up his earlier distinction between the political and social system, on the one hand, and the lifeworld of everyday, interpersonal interaction, on the other, Jürgen Habermas sees the "public sphere" as a "communication structure rooted in the lifeworld through the associational network of civil society. . . . The public sphere cannot be conceived as an institution and certainly not as an organization. It is not even a framework of norms with differentiated competences and roles, membership regulations, and so on. . . . The public sphere can best be described as a network for communicating information and points of view." The public sphere refers to "the *social space* generated in communicative action."[2] Thus the public sphere and the private sphere of the lifeworld are not distinct areas. Instead, they merge into each other in both directions. "The threshold separating the private sphere from the public is not marked by a fixed set of issues or relationships but by *different conditions of communication*. . . . they do not seal off the private from the public but only channel the flow of topics from the one sphere into the other. For the public sphere draws its impulses from the private handling of social problems that resonate in life histories."[3]

This understanding of a differentiated public space that encompasses the political system of the state, the public, political society, and civil society refers primarily to the democratically constituted community. It is not, however, simply a matter of describing the democratic political process, but of developing an analytical framework that can be generally applied in the interpretation of political systems. This is especially true for the associated concepts of power, law, and morality, as well as for the foundations of public and political legitimacy.

Max Weber defined the state as the "human community that (successfully) claims the monopoly of the legitimate use of physical force within a given territory." Politics understood as the leadership of the state, according to Weber, is essentially a matter of the exercise of power based on administrative machinery, which "successfully upholds the claim to the *monopoly* of the *legitimate* use of physical force in the enforcement of its order."[4]

Although the use of physical force or violence should be seen as a borderline case in the exercise of state power, the stress on the state monopoly of force accurately expresses the idea that political action by the state is aimed at enforcing binding decisions, with the assistance, if necessary, of force or sanctions.[5] The effectiveness of state-organized power, however, requires legitimacy through being bound into a legal system, and it is, according to Weber, the inherent rationality of the legal system that gives legitimacy to legal domination.

Behind this view of the legitimate exercise of state power is clearly the model of the secular nation-state, sovereign both internally and externally. As we saw in the previous chapter, this model emerged under the specific historical conditions of European modernity. At the same time, we noted that there was a different understanding of the political order within the political enlightenment in the Anglo-Saxon tradition. Erhard Eppler, basing his thought on the studies of the Swiss jurist Gret Haller in her book *The Limits of Atlanticism: Perceptions of State, Nation and Religion in Europe and the United States*,[6] describes the difference as follows:

> Anyone seeking to discern when the European and American understanding of the state diverged will soon arrive at 1648.... This was when the form of the modern state was set down in law, and its internal and external sovereignty defined.... Europe could end its religious wars only by giving the state the power to force the religions to arrive at peace. The United States was built by people who were hampered, even prevented, by the state from practising their religion, and who would not have tolerated anything similar in the New World. This led to an incredibly vital civil society, which only later developed a state to maintain order and security.... If Americans think of the state, they usually say, 'government'.[7]

If the European model of state-centred politics is already reaching its limits in the United States with its different historical, cultural, and religious background, so this applies even more to those societies and cultures in which political power remains bound in a web of sacral orders legitimized by tradition and custom, and where tribal loyalties, or the preservation of the community bond, take priority over enforcing and complying with formal legal norms. These are societies and cultures that have often retained a primordial sense of the fact that power cannot be reduced to an understanding of absolute power based on the relationship between giving orders and expecting (if necessary, forced) obedience. They would recognize themselves in Hannah Arendt's definition of power as "the human ability not just to act but to act in concert. Power is never the property of an individual; it belongs to a group and remains in existence only so long as the group keeps together."[8]

The concept of the public sphere and the public space outlined above builds on this notion of "communicative power" as opposed to the "strategic" or success-oriented "administrative" power of the institutional political system of the state. In his studies on the reconstruction of law, Habermas sees law as the medium "through which communicative power is translated into administrative power."[9] It emerges from the simultaneous historical development of binding law and political power, whereby "the authorization of power by sacred law and the sanctioning of law by social power are effected *uno actu* [with one action]. In this way, political power and binding law emerge as the two components that make up a legally organized political order."[10] Reflection on politics thus needs to be liberated from a fixation on the state. It must give priority to the shaping of the public space through mobilizing social and communicative power. This has consequences for the relationship between religion and politics and the understanding of the place of religion in the public space.

Religion in the Public Space: Europe

Discussions about the "return" of religion to the public space and the re-examination of secularization theory compelled us to reconsider the location and form of religion in society and to transcend the concentration, customary in the Christian context, on the "church" as a dogmatic, liturgical, and institutionally organized religious body. "Church" is a public form of religion marked by the specific developments in the history of Christianity that has no counterpart in the world's other religions. Neither in Judaism nor in Islam, quite apart from Hinduism, Buddhism, and the East Asian traditions of Confucianism, Taoism, and Shinto, is there a similar form of religion organized as a public body with a legally defined membership. Islam has the schools of the law scholars and the *umma* representing the Muslim community as a whole. It was, however, the political structure of the caliphate that guaranteed its unity, and, since the end of the caliphate, there have been only loose groupings, lacking an authority structure comparable to the church. Synagogal Judaism has a similar internal structure, although there has been some adaptation to Christian church structures, especially in the diaspora. Asian religions derive their internal structure either from monastic communities, as is the case particularly in Buddhism, or from a priesthood set apart from the believer that is responsible for ritual actions. They lack, however, a formulated doctrine and institutional structure comparable to that of Christianity.

The understanding of the public space outlined above, drawing on Habermas, encourages us to transcend the classical configuration of "church and state" in examining the place of religion in the public space. The distinction between institutional politics, the political society and civil society that has been proposed for the political public space can be applied in a similar fashion to the place of religion in this space. José Casanova thus concludes: "In principle, religion could be located, as it were, in each of these three public spaces of the polity. There may be 'public' religions at the state level, the 'church' being the paradigmatic example. There may be 'public' religions at the political society level, as in all instances when religion becomes politically mobilized against other religious or secular movements, or institutionalized as a political party competing with other religious or secular parties."[11] The third type is the form of "public" religion at the level of civil society, that is, the public space in which common normative structures, and the foundations of the "common good" are able to be clarified, critically enhanced, and reinforced through processes of social interaction and communication. This is the space of public culture. By leaving the "private" sphere to which they have been allocated by secular and functionally differentiated societies, and entering the nondifferentiated area of civil society, "religions force modern societies to reflect publicly and collectively upon their normative structures."[12] Against the background of the experience of the United States, Casanova points to three main forms of intervention: first, religious mobilization in defense of the lifeworld against various tendencies of state or market colonization; second, a critique of the allegedly "self-regulating mechanism" of the state and the market, without reference to extrinsic traditional moral norms; and third, the obstinate defense of the "common good" against liberal theories that know only the aggregated sum of individual choices.[13]

Such a typology, of course, refers to forms of public religion in modern societies. Nevertheless, it can offer an analytical framework to analyze the opportunities and limitations, strengths, and vulnerabilities of the presence of religion in the public space, as can the differentiation of the political public sphere that underlies it. In particular, such a framework helps to make clear the traditional relationship of "church" and "state" is but one borderline case of religion in the public sphere. In its classic form of the state-church, this model is now found only in a few European constitutional monarchies such as Great Britain and Denmark, the state churches of Sweden and Norway having lost this status. The process of secularization associated with the establishment of democratic state structures has paved the way for a secular understanding of the state. The recognition of the principle of the separation of church and state and of religious freedom has led to the abolition of most of the former state-church systems, especially in traditionally Catholic countries.[14]

Nevertheless, particularly in Europe, the public form of the Christian community as a "church" in the form of a public body analogous to the state has persisted. The historical process since the "Constantinian shift," whose basic features were sketched out in the previous chapter, showed that church and state structures have developed in interaction with each other, with the churches largely conforming to the dominant form of the way in which state power is organized. This applies particularly to the later form of churches as confessionally organized structures, emerging as a counterbalance to the state, which had established itself as a nation-state. Today, however, in place of the traditional close ties between church and state there are different forms of separation and of the mutual recognition of the autonomy of state and ecclesial rights and responsibilities.

At one end of the spectrum, there are states that have adopted a neutral or religiously critical attitude to religious communities. This can lead to the structural "privatization" of religion, as in principle in France, or to the all-encompassing control of religious communities by the state, as in Turkey or in the former communist states. At the other end of the spectrum are states that continue to recognize a state church, or those in which there is indeed a formal legal separation between church and state, but where the former state religion still lays claim to and receives privileges that are not granted to other religious communities (as in most Orthodox-majority countries in Eastern Europe and elsewhere).

Within this spectrum, there are many different models of institutionalized cooperation between state and church, regulated either by the country's constitution (as in Germany) or through treaties and concordats (as in Spain or Italy, for example). In most of the countries that have recently joined the European Union (such as Poland, Hungary, Slovakia, Lithuania, or Cyprus) there now exists a system in which separation of church and state is linked to a form of legally regulated cooperation. Thus the separation of church and state, as it has gradually developed in Europe since the beginning of the 20th century, does not lead ineluctably to the "privatization" of religion and the deliberate restriction of the public role of churches. Instead, the main historic churches in Europe have developed a carefully nuanced practice of "public responsibility" in recent decades. Nevertheless, the studies on secularization in Europe described in the previous chapter suggest that the public impact of institutional churches, despite their high-profile positions on key issues of political concern, has decreased significantly. Furthermore, it appears that the issue of church and state and the multiple legal forms of state and church arrangements are largely confined to the European context and cannot be applied to other regions and cultural contexts, with the exception of Latin America.[15]

This becomes particularly clear when compared to the situation in the United States. With their well-known typological distinction between the church and sect (as well as mysticism),[16] Max Weber and Ernst Troeltsch pointed out that since the time of the early church there has been a countervailing trend to that of the dominant form of the "church" as a public organization. This countervailing trend expresses critical distance to the alliance with political power, and to the claim of all-encompassing power over worldly governance. In such a perspective, the two basic types of church and sect have existed in tension throughout all phases of Christian history. This typology, which has been further developed and differentiated, may help one to comprehend the form of Christian communal relationships in the Anglo-Saxon context, particularly in the United States, which is clearly distinguishable from the European typology of the church.

In picking up and developing the approach of Weber and Troeltsch, H. Richard Niebuhr points out that the institutional form of the *denomination* developed out of movements, which can be classified as sects: "In Protestant history the sect has ever been the child of an outcast minority, taking its rise in the religious revolts of the poor, of those who were without effective representation in church or state and who formed their conventicles of dissent in the only way open to them, on the democratic, associational pattern. . . . By its very nature the sectarian type of organisation is valid only for one generation."[17] In his study, Niebuhr demonstrates that social, ethnic, cultural, or national factors have been more important in the formation of certain denominations than have questions of theology. Most of the original American denominations are the result of the consolidation of movements that began among the lower class, adapting to majority society after a few generations, and thus taking on a permanent form. The formation of denominations can thus be seen as an adaptation of the Christian community to the situation of a pluralistic society with a democratic political constitution.

The term *denomination* is secular in origin and means the designation of a specific class of objects. The concept of religious denomination takes as a given that there is a plurality of Christian communities and assumes they have equal rights as voluntary associations. In German usage the term *free church* to designate these communities has prevailed. It refers to the movements that already in the 16th century separated from the Protestant territorial churches, because they opposed the close connection between church and state, or society. They consider themselves as "free" in terms of freedom from the state, as well as in terms of their voluntary membership as a result of a conscious, personal decision. This type of "free church" has become the dominant form of Christianity in the United States. Even the churches that in Europe are organized as state or territorial churches (Roman Catholics, Anglicans, Lutherans, Presbyterians) have in the United States become *de facto* free churches. The American Methodist, Baptist, and Pentecostal denominations/ free churches, which in Europe are minority groups, are large communities in a global perspective and, especially in Asia, Africa, and Latin America, shape the profile of Protestantism. One can see the origin of denominationalism as the result of incipient secularization, that is, an explicit farewell to an all-encompassing role for the church on lines analogous to a state, and as the acceptance that civil society is the public space appropriate for the Christian community. Denominationalism is the way in which the Christian community has responded to the processes of functional social differentiation and has adapted to the specific area to which it has been assigned.

Public Religion in the United States of America

The intellectual origins of the modern principle of separation of church and state, and of religion and politics, are rooted in religious protest movements within Protestantism (Anabaptists, Baptists, and Puritans) and their struggle for liberty of faith and conscience and the freedom to practice their religion. This demand for religious freedom was a protest against the traditionally close institutional connection between church and state that continued to exist in Europe in the centuries that followed the Peace of Westphalia. The United States was the first state in which the separation of church and state was enshrined institutionally and legally, through the First Amendment to the U.S. Constitution in 1791. The first part of this article reads, "Congress shall make no law respecting an establishment of religion, or prohibiting the free exercise thereof . . ." The wording of this constitutional principle, however, arose not from specifically religious beliefs but was mainly politically motivated. It stemmed largely from Thomas Jefferson and James Madison, who were influenced by the Deistic tradition of the English Enlightenment. In a letter in 1802, Jefferson referred to a "wall of separation" between church and state. Perhaps it would be better, as Madison did thirty years later, to speak of a "line of separation" because it is less about the hermetic separation of the two spheres than about clarifying the scope of the rights of religious communities vis-à-vis those of the public authorities—something that continually needs to be undertaken anew. The adoption of this amendment to the Constitution, however, was preceded by a long debate within and between the various colonies. The Congregationalist descendants of the Puritans in New England sought a quasi-theocratic order. The Anglicans in the southern states wanted to maintain the state-church constitution of the Church of England. The colony of Rhode Island founded by the Baptist Roger Williams already made the issue of religious freedom and the separation of church and state a constitutional principle in 1640. This position slowly prevailed in the ensuing period, although for Jefferson and Madison it was a question of limiting and overcoming the conflicts that had resulted and continued to result from the potential amalgam of religion and politics.[18]

Behind this constitutional principle was a secular understanding of the state. This did not mean, however, that religion was seen as a matter solely for individual conviction without relevance for the life of society. From the very beginning, the founding of the United States was seen as an event resulting from the action of God. The separation of church and state does not mean that God as the all-powerful sovereign should be kept out of the political process. On the contrary: the foundational myth of the United States sees God's direct action in American history, on the pattern of the exodus of Israel from slavery in Egypt. America is the new promised land and is called to be a "light unto the nations." Even though the Constitution does not contain explicit reference to God, the religious dimension of American collective identity is clearly expressed in the motto "In God we trust," which is found on every dollar bill, and in the formulation of the "Pledge of Allegiance," a patriotic declaration of loyalty recited on public occasions and in schools before the beginning of class, as well as in the reference to being "one nation under God." One can also point to the public invocation of God in the expressions "God bless America" or "God save the United States."

There has been a lively discussion about the nature of this "public religion" since the publication of Robert N. Bellah's famous essay "Civil Religion in America."[19] Using the Rousseauian concept of "civil religion," Bellah elaborates the basic elements, symbols, and rituals of "public religion" in the United States and traces their origins back to the declarations and speeches of the founding fathers of the United States. It becomes clear that this is an understanding and practice of religion that largely avoids explicit reference to particular religious traditions. Instead, a general, nonspecific invocation of God and symbolic and ritual functions, including national holidays such as Independence Day, Memorial Day, or Thanksgiving Day, serve as a religious basis for continually reintegrating a thoroughly pluralistic society. It is a kind of "republican religion" (Tocqueville) that creates a public space within which different religious groups and traditions are able to contribute to public debate as they think best and without state control. This is the basis of the specific relationship between religion and politics in the United States, which is markedly different from the situation in most European countries.

Bellah himself refers in his essay to the danger of civil religion being misused to legitimize the pursuit of imperial state power through the use of terms such as "manifest destiny" and God's "covenant" with America. In later publications, he concludes that the national "covenant" has been broken.[20] This danger is particularly acute where sectional religious interests, such as evangelical fundamentalism, seek to use the concept of civil religion, which then takes on a "theocratic" character, or becomes a public religion at the level of the state (see chap. 4, below). In any case, Bellah warns against making the analytical concept of "civil religion" a normative concept in the sense of civil religion becoming the prerequisite for the functional integration of a society. José Casanova, in his earlier-mentioned book, takes a similarly critical standpoint: "What needs to be examined is the different ways in which religions, old and new, traditional and modern, may play public roles, eufunctional and dysfunctional, in the public sphere of civil society. Consequently, the concept of 'civil religion' ought to be reformulated from the state or societal community level to the level of civil society."[21]

Public Religion in Postcolonial States

As a result of colonialism and the processes of modernization, the secular nation-state has become the basic model of state order in most countries of the southern hemisphere. It has superseded, though not completely replaced, older models in which religious tradition and political governance are closely connected. This has led to the tensions that continue to shape the political life and public role of religion.[22] In many cases, particularly in Africa, the borders of the new nation-states drawn according to the interests of the colonial powers have proved to be arbitrary, because they separate originally contiguous ethnic and cultural entities. In Islamic countries the enforced separation of the Muslim community into different nation-states by the colonial powers has been perceived as being in contradiction to and an attack on the unity of the *umma*. But even in countries whose "national" unity existed independently of colonialism, such as India, Sri Lanka, or Thailand, there is ethnically or religiously motivated opposition to the secular conception of the state. As a result of centuries of migration and of mission by Christians and Muslims, as well as by Buddhists and Hindus, most of the countries have been marked by religious pluralism, which sometimes leads to mutual adaptation and the mingling of traditions at the level of the lifeworld, but may also result in a struggle for hegemony and influence at the public level of society.

The typological differentiation between various forms of public religion in relation to the institutional political system, that is, the state, political society, or civil society, has only limited application to such situations. In particular, many of these countries lack an independent civil society and thus the vital prerequisite for the communicative structure of the public sphere. We are frequently dealing with state structures that, despite the formal achievement of democratization, maintain a universal claim to power and thus come into conflict—repeatedly and increasingly—with the public demands of religious traditions. The economic, political, and cultural effects of globalization have exacerbated the tensions and conflicts between religion and politics in many countries and have led to the formation of new religiously based movements and parties, which within the framework of political society take part in the debate about the orientation and identity of the community as a whole. They are adopting a form of public religion that in similar cultural and political conflicts of an earlier time in Europe (and to a lesser extent in Latin America) led to the formation of Christian parties and initiatives such as Catholic Action. These new religious movements, which are acting specifically in the arena of political society, are found also in Muslim, Hindu, Buddhist, and Jewish-influenced countries and regions. They are often described, particularly in the United States, as "fundamentalist," on the model of Christian fundamentalist movements. This term is rather misleading, as a more detailed analysis of fundamentalism in chapter 4 will show. What unites most of these movements is their resistance to the modern, secular understanding of the political and social order with a tendency, at the very least, toward the privatization of religion. In many cases, the aspiration of restoring the traditional public role of religion is closely linked to the struggle for national (and ethnic) identity, which in religiously pluralistic contexts can result in violent conflict.[23]

The studies by Juergensmeyer, Gilles Kepel, Jeff Haynes, and Peter Beyer that were discussed in the previous chapter offer a more detailed analysis of these kinds of movements in a number of countries. The study by Haynes provides detailed historical and contemporary research on the developments in the relationship between religion and politics in almost all regions and continents, such as the United States, Latin America, and Europe, via Africa and the Middle East to Central Asia, India, and Southeast Asia.[24] It is beyond the scope of this chapter to attempt to summarize his detailed observations. The following chapters will discuss the role of Muslim and Islamist movements and the influence of fundamentalism in the United States and worldwide. Here we shall look at the situation in South and Southeast Asia with their plurality of ancient religious traditions and their public profile.

The three forms of political religion in Asia described below represent the three most important religious traditions in Asia, namely Hinduism, Islam, and Buddhism. The first example is *India*, which according to its constitution is a secular state that offers equal respect to all religions and ensures the protection of minorities, going back to the political and religious convictions of Mahatma Gandhi. Under India's first prime minister, Jawaharlal Nehru, the secular nature of the Indian state was linked to the development of a modern, democratic society, initially receiving wide support given the experience of the violent conflicts between Hindus and Muslims that preceded independence. In the years that followed, Hindu nationalist movements gained in importance, leading to the founding in 1964 of the *Vishva Hindu Parishad* (World Hindu Council) and of the *Bharatiya Janata Party* (Indian People's Party) in 1980, a political party that formed the federal government from 1998 to 2004, and makes up several state governments. India thus offers an example of public religious activity at the level of the political society up to and including assuming power in the institutional political system.

The second example is *Indonesia*, which, with 190 million Muslims, has the world's largest Islamic population. Alongside Islam, Indonesia recognizes Catholicism, Protestantism, Hinduism, Buddhism, and Confucianism as official religions. As the basis for building the new state of Indonesia following Dutch colonialism, the country's first president, Sukharno, introduced the five principles of *Pancasila* into the constitution: belief in the one and only God; just and civilized humanity; the unity of Indonesia; democracy guided by the inner wisdom in the unanimity arising out of deliberations amongst representatives; and social justice for all of the people of Indonesia. Through a 1985 law, *Pancasila* was declared a state ideology, thus becoming a form of civil religion that is binding on all holders of public office as well as in school and university education. From the very beginning, there were movements that tried to tie Indonesia more strongly to Islamic principles and to suppress the influence of other religious traditions, although the largest

Muslim organizations concentrated their activity by contrast in the social arena, thus an area of civil society where religious plurality is particularly marked. Despite all the political crises and processes of transformation, the social order based on *Pancasila* has proved remarkably resilient and able to resist religious extremism. Indonesia thus offers an example of a public praxis of religion in a situation of religious pluralism, supported by an officially formulated consensus about values. Indonesia also demonstrates that religious traditions are able to assume a key role in the creation of an autonomous civil society.

The third form of public religion is that of the Buddhist-majority countries of *Burma, Thailand, and Sri Lanka*. Buddhism has its origins in India and became the dominant religion in the 2nd century BCE under King Ashoka, whose rule, based on the ethical principles of Buddhism, became an idealized model for the relationship between religion and politics in the neighbouring countries where Buddhism developed. Thus the monarchy and the hierarchy of the Buddhist community of monks were closely linked in the precolonial societies of Burma, Thailand, Cambodia, and Sri Lanka. Thailand alone was not affected by Western colonialism and thus preserved the traditionally close relationship between the monarchy and the Buddhist leaders. At the same time, Thailand has been most directly affected by economic and social modernization and since the 1970s groups of younger people have been at the forefront of challenging the traditional Buddhist hierarchy monks, often alongside radical student groups. In Burma, the connection between the monarchy and the Buddhist hierarchy was broken under British colonialism, but Buddhism, comprising about 80 percent of the population, remained a factor in public life. Though the first post-independence governments tried to rebuild this connection the military regime that followed began by repressing Buddhism in order to transform Burma into a secular, socialist state. Since 2008, groups of younger monks have become one of the motors of resistance against the military dictatorship. In Sri Lanka, Buddhism has been rooted in the Sinhalase majority since the time of King

Ashoka. A reform movement within Buddhism directed toward education and social involvement began in the 19th century, gaining influence among monks and laity; this prepared the ground for the later development of "communalism," according to which social groups are identified on the basis of religion. Sri Lanka is more marked by ethnic and religious pluralism than the other countries mentioned in this section. Thus the ethnic and religious conflicts between Tamils and Sinhalese were exacerbated by the actions of radial nationalist movements of Buddhist monks, who rejected any compromise with the then Tamil minority. The National Heritage Party (JHU), founded in 2004 and composed exclusively of monks, aims to make Buddhism the state religion and to institute a Buddhist state.

The three profiles of public religion that have been briefly outlined here are very different. What unites them is the fact that religion in all five states has exerted and continues to exert a determining public influence on the political community in the postcolonial period. This is not so much the issue of the "resurgence" of religious traditions, because these traditions had continued to exist during the colonial period, at least in the lifeworld of the people. Rather, it demonstrates the powerful role of religion in the collective identity of society. The secular state system in India is intended to ensure equal rights and opportunities for the different religions, but it is being exposed to increasing pressure from nationalist movements with a religious background that oppose the separation of religion and politics and that marginalize ethnic and religious minorities. Indonesia has chosen the path of introducing a kind of civil religion in the form of *Pancasila* and has officially recognized six religious traditions. This state integration of religious pluralism has not been able to prevent Islamist extremism. It has, however, opened up a space within civil society for public religion that is not primarily about political influence and access to state power, but about the normative cohesion of society. The Buddhist countries are faced with the task of transforming the traditionally close mutual bonds between state and religion into a system in which both the state and the Buddhist hierarchy of monastic communities are open to the social transformations that are needed and through which the authoritarian exercise of power may be overcome. The Buddhist reform movements of monks and laypeople who act within both political society and the emerging civil society are committed to defending national-religious identity, but in the context of Buddhist tradition they represent a new form of public religion. Above all, they demonstrate that religious traditions continue to represent an important basis for the legitimacy of political power structures, whether in the form of a general civil religion, or in the form of a state ideology.

The Debate about Religious Freedom

In considering the situation in India, Jeff Haynes indirectly refers to the issue of religious freedom, which is a matter of central importance in situations of religious pluralism. Although a certain political consensus has emerged on the issue of religious freedom during the past 60 years, it remains controversial. Article 19 of the 1948 Universal Declaration of Human Rights states: "Everyone has the right to freedom of thought, conscience and religion; this right includes freedom to change his religion or belief, and freedom, either alone or in community with others and in public or private, to manifest his religion or belief in teaching, practice, worship and observance." This is still the most far-reaching formulation of the principle of religious freedom, but is still only a statement of intent. Almost 20 years later, the provisions in legally binding form of the 1966 International Covenant on Civil and Political Rights seem a little more cautious, a trend that continues in the Declaration of the General Assembly of the United Nations from 1981 on the "Elimination of all Forms of Intolerance and of Discrimination Based on Religion or Belief." The change in wording, from the right to "change" one's religion, to the right to "have and adopt" a religion, and then to the lapidary right to "have" a religion, shows just how controversial the implications of the principle of religious freedom still are.

The dissidents from Anabaptist and Calvinist Protestantism who emigrated to America were struggling for their religious freedom. The principle was adopted only slowly and with hesitation in European states and their majority churches. Only with the declaration *Dignitatis Humanae* of the Second Vatican Council did the Roman Catholic Church adopt this principle. In general it can be said that it was mainly governments and intergovernmental organizations that established the right to freedom of religion. Religious communities themselves disregarded or even opposed the principle, especially in situations where they were in the majority compared to other religions.[25]

The separation of church and state, and the secular understanding of government and politics that accompanies it, is usually seen as a prerequisite for the realization of full religious freedom. As the survey above has shown, such separation of church and state may differ in its significance and the form that it takes. It may be tolerant of or at least take a neutral attitude toward religious communities and their presence in the life of society. Politics may try to keep religion as far away as possible from public life and banish it to the private sphere. In extreme cases, the separation of religion and politics can also lead to significant state control over the activities of religious communities, ranging from mandatory registration, via the withdrawal of legal existence, the transfer of church property into public hands and making clergy part of the state apparatus, to limiting religious freedom to the mere freedom of belief and conscience. Wherever government policy seeks to exercise a universal claim to sovereignty over all areas of public life, it will be suspicious of the influence of religion and the power it exercises on the consciousness and behaviour of people, and it will try to neutralize this rival source of power. One example is the practice of governments in the former communist states. Freedom of religion proves to be an important, albeit not sufficient, condition for the constitution of an independent public space over against the claims of dominance by the state.

For the sake of the transparency and legitimacy of political order and for the credibility and integrity of religion, we cannot dispense with the modern distinction between the two spheres of religion and politics, while not seeing them as being completely separate from each other. Here the principle of religious freedom has its inalienable place. However, the way in which the two spheres are related to each other has to be continually redetermined, with the legal and institutional model of "church" and "state" having only limited application. Instead, it is important to give more attention to the "public space" as a field of interaction between religion and politics, both in the dialogue between religions and with those holding political responsibility. The "public space" needs to be protected in its own right against the hegemonic claims of institutional politics as well as any tendencies to dominate by a particular secular- or religious-based culture. This is also and above all the case for religions with their publicly orientated message and praxis. Their place is in public communication about the conditions and sustainability of the human community rather than in the debate about the assertion and exercise of political power or the competition for the growth of adherents or believers. The "public space" so understood is a place of equality without institutional or legal privileges, and where freedom of religion is a fundamental instrument for its protection. This is where the issues of legitimacy and the objectives of political authority and exercise of power need to be dealt with in a critical discourse; this is where pluralistic religious traditions may articulate their public role. A "public religion" that sees itself as a "custodian" of this space is able to resist the temptation to take part in the power of political decision making, and it gains strength and confidence to reject any attempt to be exploited for political or ethnic and nationalist interests and goals.

3. Religion and Politics in Islam

The Return of Islam to the Political Stage

One of the main reasons for the new debate about religion and politics is the "renaissance" of Islam and its undeniable entry into the international public space. There is now a firmly established belief within the Western public that religion and politics are inseparably linked in Islam, and that the concept of a secular state with a democratic constitution and legal order is incompatible with Islamic tradition. In particular, the demands in many Muslim-majority countries for *sharia* to become the basis of public law have led to fear and hostility, and have nourished negative stereotypes about Islam. The issue of the relationship between religion and politics certainly plays a central role in current attempts to refound and reaffirm the identity of the Muslim community within a global context. A closer examination of the Muslim world, however, illustrates the conclusion of the second chapter that "all religions under the pressure of the process of globalization are forced to reflect in a new and critical way on the relationship between religion and politics." In so doing, it becomes clear that attempting to single out the Islamic tradition by claiming that it is founded on the unity of religion and politics does not stand up to impartial scrutiny.

With the end of the Ottoman Empire 90 years ago, it seemed that Islam had departed from the global political stage on which at times it played a formative role. Turkey, as the heartland of the

Ottoman Empire, was transformed under Mustafa Kemal into a secular, laicistic republic. The abolition of the sultanate in 1924 put an end to the tradition—interrupted several times but in essence going back through the centuries to Muhammad—of the caliphate as a visible, symbolic point of reference for the unity of the Muslim community and its political form.

The remaining provinces of the Ottoman Empire in the Middle East were placed as protectorates under the administration of France and Britain by the Sykes-Picot Agreement of 1916. As early as 1902, the areas of the Arabian peninsula controlled by the Saud dynasty were liberated from Ottoman control and became independent in 1932 as the Kingdom of Saudi Arabia. Egypt, which had been part of the Ottoman Empire until the expedition of Napoleon (1798–1802) and which until 1922 was a British protectorate following the construction of the Suez Canal, became a sovereign state in 1936. In 1932, Iraq was accepted into the League of Nations, followed by Lebanon (1943) and (Trans)Jordan and Syria (both in 1946). Thus were finally dashed the hopes founded on vague British promises that a Greater Arabia would be formed from the Arab provinces of the Ottoman Empire, thereby restoring the unity of the Arab Islamic community. The ancient Muslim areas in the Middle East and North Africa were compelled by the political decisions of the colonial and protectorate powers to constitute themselves as independent nation-states and to redetermine the relationship between their citizens and their cultural and religious identity.

The concept of Pan-Islamism developed among intellectuals in the Ottoman Empire and in India as far back as the 19th century in response to the European penetration of the Islamic world. For a short time during the final phase of the Ottoman Empire, Pan-Islamism became the state ideology as a counter to Turkish nationalism. After the end of the caliphate, a series of conferences attempted to transform the Pan-Islamic ideal into more solid structures. This attempt, however, was unable to prevail against the competing trend of Pan-Arabism, which gained organizational expression with the founding of the Arab League in 1945.

Both movements aimed to liberate Islam and the countries with an Islamic tradition from the influence of the European colonial powers and to give them a voice of their own in the world. Two factors were and are of paramount importance for what followed. The first was the creation of Israel in 1948 in the former British Mandate Territory of Palestine, leading to the recurring armed conflicts between Israel and its Arab neighbours, which ended in ceasefires or defeat for the Arab states. Opposition to Israel, as a state supported by Europe and the United States, became a catalyst for the politicization of Islam at an international level, and strengthened efforts for Pan-Islamic solidarity and cooperation. The second important factor was the increase in the geopolitical power of the oil-rich Islamic countries in the Persian Gulf through the establishment of OPEC in 1960 and the oil crisis that was unleashed as a response to the Yom Kippur War of 1973. Through its revenues from oil exports, Saudi Arabia was in a position to steadily promote its own interests based on Islamic expansionism. In 1962, the League of the Islamic World was constituted in Mecca as a nongovernmental organization, founded by Muslim intellectuals to represent the cultural and religious interests of the Islamic peoples, and supported by Saudi Arabia. Through its dependence on Saudi Arabia, it serves primarily as an instrument for the dissemination of the traditionalist-conservative principles of the Saudi form of Wahhabi Islam.

More important than the League of the Islamic World is the Organisation of the Islamic Conference (OIC), founded in 1969 in Rabat by 22 Islamic states, initially intended as a direct response to the annexation of East Jerusalem by Israel after the Six-Day War of 1967. The OIC has meanwhile become a major international political representative of the Islamic countries, with 57 member states and a secretariat in Jeddah. The goals adopted at the 1972 Conference of Foreign Ministers are aimed at promoting Islamic solidarity and broad cooperation between member states. The conference promotes the rights and dignity of all Muslims and aims to overcome all forms of racial discrimination and colonialism. The OIC "Cairo

Declaration on Human Rights in Islam," adopted by the Conference of Foreign Ministers in 1990, requires particular attention. In Article 24 and 25, it defines *sharia* as the sole basis of human rights, thereby reaffirming the critique of the Universal Declaration of Human Rights that was advanced by Saudi Arabia when the declaration was adopted in 1948. In the preamble to the Cairo Declaration the member states of the OIC say that they are "Reaffirming the civilizing and historical role of the Islamic Ummah which God made the best nation that has given mankind a universal and well-balanced civilization."[1] Recently, at the insistence of Pakistan the OIC has also demanded that the "defamation of religion" be subject internationally to criminal sanctions.

The specific form of the way in which politics and religion are connected in the Islamic world, and which contrasts with the Western concept of the secular state, is also reflected in various approaches to the theory and constitutional structure of an Islamic state. The first model was created in the 18th century with the treaty between the emir and the Saudi Wahhabis to consolidate rule in the Arabian Peninsula. The Kingdom of Saudi Arabia was formally established in 1932 as the first Islamic state, not only declaring Islam the sole state religion, but also giving constitutional status to the Qur'an and the Sunnah of the Prophet. With the partition of India at the end of British colonial rule, the newly created Pakistan was faced with the task of clarifying its Islamic identity. The 1952 constitution made Pakistan the world's first "Islamic Republic." The amended constitution of 1962 following the 1958 military coup weakened the Islamic nature of the state. A further amendment to the constitution in 1973 declaring Islam as the state religion, and including aspirations for a greater Islamization of the country, including *sharia* as the basis of law, have since become the focus of still unresolved political conflict in Pakistan.

The 1979 revolution in Iran created a huge international furor by ending the authoritarian regime of the Shah which had aimed at forced modernization and establishing an "Islamic Republic" on the basis of Shiite tradition. There was a lively debate in Iran from the beginning of the 20th century among legal and religious scholars on the Islamic principles of constitutionality and the relationship between religion and politics in an Islamic state. The constitution of the Islamic Republic of Iran combines the basic elements of a presidential democracy with the Shiite tradition of the higher authority of the legal scholars as represented by the Supreme Leader and the Council of Guardians.

The successful Islamic revolution in Iran strengthened the confidence of movements of political Islam in all Islamic countries. Today, Islam is recognized as a state religion in 22 states: all of the traditionally Islamic countries in the Middle East and North Africa as well as Pakistan, Bangladesh, Malaysia, Iraq, and Iran. The substantive determination of the Islamic identity of the states remains a highly controversial area of political debate. The movements of militant Islamism, which, despite all their differences over details, are united in the aim of forming an Islamic state based on *sharia* law, are increasingly responsible for the way in which the Islamic world is seen from outside. Nevertheless, on closer inspection it becomes clear that the content and religious as well as the political definition of the concept of an Islamic state is highly controversial.

Against this background, it is necessary to examine more closely the tradition and historical development of the relationship between religion and politics in Islam, and to evaluate the different approaches at reform that are aimed at a critical reappropriation of tradition to formulate genuine Islamic answers to current social and political challenges.

The basis of the Islamic legal system is *sharia*, which in the Qur'an is described as the "the path" or "the way" (45:18). In the form it was received under the Abbasid dynasty, it includes all of the legislation required for the lives of Muslims: religious and social rules, political and economic principles, and ethical and legal standards. *Sharia* is based on two basic sources, namely the Qur'an and the Sunnah. Since the Qur'an is mostly made up of religious and cultic regulations and ethical teachings, but only a few legal definitions in the strict sense, the Sunnah became the main source of development of *sharia*. Unlike other legal systems, however, *sharia* has never been codified. Although it is an authoritative point of reference for the shape of an Islamic social order, it is also the subject of unfinished discussions and conflicts as far as its correct interpretation and practical application are concerned, and in particular whether *sharia* is to be understood as "sacred," justified by divine revelation, and thus immutable law. However, there is agreement about the basic direction and aims of *sharia*: the focus is on the realization of social justice and equality, promoting the welfare of the community and its members. These are, of course, also the goals and basic values of the Qur'an itself, and *sharia* is thus the path to achieve these goals and not an end in itself. This character of *sharia* is distorted if it is reduced to "harsh punishment laws."[2]

Sharia itself is the result of a process of development that reached an interim conclusion only in the Abbasid period. This is especially true for the second source of *sharia* law, the Sunnah, meaning "tradition," which originally denoted the local customs in the various regions of the Islamic empire. A higher legal tradition had emerged through the decisions of the caliphs and the qadis they appointed, which needed to be reconciled with the objectives and ethical standards of the Qur'an and the collective tradition of the deeds and words of the Prophet (*hadith*). This was the task which the group of legal experts that grew up toward the end of the Umayyad period set themselves. The Abbasid caliphs, who wanted to be guided by Islamic law in their rule, gave a publicly recognized status to the guild of lawyers (*fuqaha*), who received the task of interpreting Islamic law and monitoring its application by interpreting the sources, that is, the Qur'an and the Sunnah, and by systematizing the legal decisions that had been handed down.

The role of authoritative interpretation began with the sources, and especially the Sunnah. The "Sunnah of the Prophet" now meant all of the words, deeds, and decisions of the Prophet Muhammad that had been handed down. Early on, until the middle of the 9th century, they were only transmitted orally as hadiths, that is, individual reports. From the 9th century onward, as the oral tradition was not reliable enough, the hadiths that were circulating began to be collected and their authenticity verified, that is, whether they had an actual connection with the life and work of the Prophet. The first and most important of these collections remains to this day that of al-Bukhari (810–870), an Islamic scholar who was active in what is now Uzbekistan.

Of course, not all questions of law could be settled by reference to the sources, the Qur'an and the Sunnah. The legal scholars were thus obliged to use their own intellect and reason (*ijtihad*) to develop rules that were in the spirit of *sharia*. Using argument by analogy (*qiyas*), the formulation of new rules in accordance with accepted principles was recognized as a legitimate method for specific legal decisions. Certainly, ultimate authority could be claimed only by those legal principles that were supported by the consensus (*ijma*) of the community, but in practice this meant that they could be based on the consensus of the legal scholars.

The various schools of legal scholars thus took on central importance in the formulation of Islamic law and for the binding interpretation of *sharia*.[3] They differed in the weight they gave to the basic rules of Islamic jurisprudence as sketched out above. The oldest of these schools, the Hanafite, is attributed to Abu Hanifa from Kufa (699–767). Its doctrine was the basis for the legal system of the Abbasid dynasty and for the later Ottoman Empire. It is widespread today in Turkey, in Sunni Iraq, in Syria and Egypt, as well as in India, Pakistan, and Central Asia. The key sources of law for the Hanafite are the Qur'an and the hadith that are recognized as authentic. They may be interpreted through analogy and by the reasonable opinion of the judge (*ra'y*). Thus, in addition to the authoritative sources, the Hanafite create space for "sound judgment" (*gesunder Menschenverstand*),[4] which lends this tradition a certain degree of flexibility, coupled with the ability to find an appropriate response to new legal issues.

The second ancient school, that of the Malikite, goes back to the lawyer Malik (710–795) from Medina. Malik wrote the first manual of Islamic law, in which he adhered strictly to the dominant tradition in Medina. He also recognized the importance of analogy and the opinion of the judge, but adhered mainly to the consensus of the community of Medina and the prevailing legal practice there. Thus the Malikite school became a model for a conservative interpretation of the law. Its influence extended from Arabia to Egypt to Spain and still today determines the Islamic legal discussion in the Maghreb, Upper Egypt, the Gulf states, Sudan, and Nigeria.

A generation later, the jurist Idris ash-Shafi'i (767–820), born in Palestine, and later active in Baghdad and Egypt, founded the school of the Shafi'i. In his main work he gathered together the recognized formal rules and methods of Islamic jurisprudence into a systematic legal framework and succeeded in mediating between the liberal tradition of the Hanafite and the conservatism of the Malikite. He limited jurisprudence to the four sources already mentioned, that is, the Qu'ran, the Sunnah (*hadith*), analogy, and the consensus of the community. He rejected the possibility of a more independent judgment by judges. The Sunnah, however, took on an importance almost equivalent to that of the Qu'ran, whereas analogy and the appeal to the consensus of the community held a lesser position. Thus tradition became the crucial principle. The Sunnah of the Prophet, like the Qu'ran, was given the authority of divine inspiration, and tight limits were placed on its interpretation. The Shafi'i legal school was influential in Egypt in particular and is now widespread in Upper Egypt, Syria, East Africa, and Southeast Asia.

Still later, Ahmad ibn Hanbal (780–855), from Baghdad, founded the fourth of the great law schools, that of the Hanbalite. He referred explicitly to the teachings of ash-Shafi'i, but accused him of having given still too much space to rational interpretation in the form of analogy and the independent judgment of the judge. He therefore bound jurisprudence to the literal interpretation of the Qur'an and the Sunnah of the Prophet. This rigorous and puritanical view was widespread in Syria and Iraq until the reign of the Ottomans and was later adopted by the Wahhabis in Saudi Arabia, where it is still important.

This brief overview makes clear that a conservative and traditionalist view of Islamic law prevailed during Abbasid rule. As a result, the practice of using independent insight and the reasonable judgment of the legal scholars as a legitimate way of discerning jurisprudence that had been necessary for the development of the Sunnah, and had been expressly advocated by the Hanafite, was increasingly relegated in importance compared to the tradition of the Prophet that became the authoritative standard. Thus the view developed in Sunni Islam that the "gate of *ijtihad*," the possibility of further development of Islamic law by rational argument on the basis of reason, had been closed since the end of the 9th century. This was the starting point for the intra-Islamic debate on reform that began in the mid-19th century. It was also inspired by the fact that the Shiite tradition not only regarded the principle of *ijtihad* as legitimate, but as "a permanent, imperative duty of the learned as the principal means of extracting the religious rules from the Quran, the Tradition and the consensus."[5] Shiite jurisprudence is based on the sources already mentioned, that is, the Qur'an and the tradition; the place of the principle of analogy is taken by the indispensable use of reason, and the consensus of the community is valid only when it carries the authority of the imam, or his representative, the *ulama*.

A more nuanced understanding of the Islamic legal system is thus of crucial importance when it comes to dealing with the relationship between religion and politics in Islam. Islamic experts today stress the necessity of distinguishing between *sharia*, as the God-given path toward a pleasing life in the community, and the formulation of Islamic law (*fiqh*), which is a human interpretation of the objectives of *sharia*, and depends upon historical and social conditions. The political order of the Islamic community was based upon the paramount role of the caliph as a representative of the Prophet. Like all Muslims, the caliphs were subject to the principles of *sharia*, on which good and fair governance was to be based. The legitimacy of the governance of the caliphs was tied to their obligation to ensure an order that corresponded to *sharia*. Nevertheless, the interpretation and the exegesis of *sharia* and the formulation of the rules of Islamic law remained in the hands of the legal scholars in the schools described above. The legislative authority of the caliph was thus limited and bound by the decisions of the legal scholars. They were the guardians of the Islamic tradition, and thus, at least potentially, a counterbalance to the caliphs and their administration of the empire.

One may debate whether or not the caliphate actually constituted a "theocratic" form of government. If what is meant by theocracy is that political governance is subject to the sovereignty of God's will and the authority of his appointed interpreter, then the Abbasid caliphate may indeed represent a form of theocracy. This does not mean, however, an undifferentiated unity of religion and politics, as demonstrated by the clearly distinct roles of the caliph, his viziers, and governors on the one hand, and the legal scholars on the other. Since the legitimacy of the rule of the caliphs was bound to the objectives of *sharia*, however, there was a tendency to bind the legal scholars as closely as possible to the ruling apparatus and to restrict their original independence. The role of being a critical counterbalance gradually became subservient to a system of "court lawyers," which was unable to prevent the subsequent decline of the Abbasid rule and the transition to the pure power politics of the rulers in the largely independent provinces of the empire.

Dissolution of the Traditional Order and Reform Movements

The Mongol invasion of 1258 sealed the fate of the Abbasid dynasty, their power having been devolved *de facto* to the rulers of the autonomous provinces three centuries earlier. The subsequent period of the Islamic Middle Ages was marked by the traditionalism of the great law schools on one hand and by the mystical Islam of the Sufis on the other. This mystical Islam mainly spread among simple country people and developed close links to popular religious traditions. At the same time an autonomous Muslim theology developed through the encounter with the legacy of Greek philosophy, which, in conjunction with the great flowering of Islamic culture in Andalusia, Spain, also influenced medieval Christian theology.[6]

After the failure of the crusades of the Christian rulers of the West and the conquest of Byzantium by the Ottomans in 1453, Sultan Selim I (1512–1520) was able to build up an Ottoman Empire that could take the place of the previous Islamic empires and thus revive the tradition of the caliphate. Alongside the Ottoman Empire in the west of the Muslim world, Islamic empires emerged at the same time in India, in the shape of the Mughal Empire, which reached its peak under Akkbar (1542–1605), and the Safavid Empire in Persia, in which Shiite Islam became the state religion. All three empires represented significant attempts to develop political systems based on the traditions of Islam, and were obliged to bring the requirements of effective political power into conformity with the rules and principles of Islamic law. The guardians of legal tradition (*ulama*), especially in Persia and the Ottoman Empire, were closely linked to the political rulers and incorporated into the state apparatus, thereby losing many of their critical functions, and instead serving mainly to legitimize the existing order.

The intra-Islamic reform movements developed as a result of conflict with Western modernity and the intrusion of colonialism into the Islamic world. In India, Britain took over direct rule as a colonial power after the crushing of the Sepoy rebellion in 1857. The Safavid Empire in Persia also came under the control of foreign powers: Russia in the north and Britain in the south. In Egypt, Ottoman rule was ended by the advance of Napoleon in 1798, and increasing British influence through the construction of the Suez Canal was consolidated in the form of a protectorate administration in the late 19th century. The Ottoman Empire alone managed to maintain its political independence until the end of the First World War, even if it had been obliged to cede significant territories and had been pushed back to the area of present-day Turkey and the Arab provinces in previous clashes with the Western powers, particularly Britain and France, and Russia.

The first influential figure of the reform movement in the second half of the 19th century was the Indian scholar Sayyid Ahmad Khan (1817–1898). By adopting European education and culture, he attempted to develop a modern, enlightened understanding of Islam and to convince the British colonial power that Islam is compatible with modernity. His appeal for the separation of religion and politics, however, failed to gain the support of his contemporaries. In the struggle against colonialism the concept of an Islamic state took on greater importance, as later demonstrated in Pakistan by Abul Ala Mawdudi (1903–1979) and the Jamaat-i-Islami movement he founded. We shall return to this in the next section.

The real founder of Islamic modernism is Jamal ad-Din al-Afghani (1838–1897), born in Iran. In an unsettled life, which led him to Afghanistan, India, Istanbul, Turkey, Egypt, Europe, and finally Istanbul, he campaigned tirelessly for the concept of Pan-Islamic unity and for a reformed and modernized Islam that would adopt Western science and technology. He believed that Western culture is not a necessary condition for scientific and technical development and that a reform of orthodox, traditionalist Islam would offer Islamic countries a means for the modern development of society, free from colonial dependency.

During his long stay in Egypt he came in contact with Muhammad Abduh (1849–1905), one of the legal and religious scholars trained at Al-Azhar University in Cairo. Abduh initially worked as a university teacher and journalist, and despite many conflicts with the government and legal scholars at the Al-Azhar University, was later appointed Mufti of Egypt. Like al-Afghani, his pupil and friend, Abduh was engaged in resistance against British colonial rule and was exiled for a time. In their reform ideas, they both sought to return an Islam mired in traditionalism to the original ideas and principles of Muhammad and his immediate successors, the "rightly guided" first four caliphs. This focus on an idealized original Islam of the ancestors has become known as Salafism. In contrast to the fundamentalist tenor of Salafi in Wahhabi Saudi Arabia, Afghani and Abduh sought to combine reason and revelation, and through a new "opening of the gates of *ijtihad*," to reinterpret the sources of the Qur'an and the Sunnah, and thus the Islamic order of *sharia* rules, for the requirements of a modern society. Abduh's position as Mufti allowed him to initiate a judicial reform in Egypt. He advocated separating the functions of the state from the role of the legal scholars, to allow the renewal of Islamic law, distinguishing between the religious duties to God that remained valid and historically changeable rules for coexisting in the community.

The liberal, Pan-Islamist ideas of al-Afghani and Abduh, despite their strong appeal propagated through various publications, were unable to prevail against opposition from conservative legal scholars and the secular nationalism that was gaining in strength. Thus Abduh's pupil Rashid Rida (1865–1935), a journalist originally from Beirut, transformed the doctrine of the return to the sources into an ideological break with the West. After the end of the Ottoman Empire, he advocated the establishment of an Islamic state and became a pioneer of political Islam, focused on the revival of Islamic values, isolated from the influences of Western modernity.

The Question of Islamism

The decisive date for the development of political Islam was the transformation of Turkey into a secular republic and the abolition of the caliphate in 1924.[7] The caliphate had long lost its original significance, both religious and political, for the unity of the Muslim world. Even Islamic historians admit that the legitimacy of most caliphs, after the initial period of the four "rightly guided" caliphs, was not in strict compliance with the rules of Islamic tradition but, rather, founded on their political power, often acquired through intrigue or obtained by force. As long as they could effectively defend their sovereignty externally and internally, and ensure a measure of security and well-being for the population, they were regarded as the rightful successors of the Prophet and, with a few exceptions, were able to maintain the support of the guardians of the Islamic tradition and the law. Their actions as legislators, which often ignored the principles of Islamic law, were tolerated or justified as being the inevitable necessity of maintaining the political order. It would therefore be historically incorrect to speak of religion and politics forming an inseparable unity in Islam. Instead, there was a pragmatic differentiation between the two spheres, even if the idea of the role of tradition in encompassing all areas of life, and in particular the role of traditional *sharia* law, was maintained. There was, however, never an authoritative interpretation of *sharia* equally binding on all Muslim communities, and often the religious institutions responsible for the formation and application of Islamic law were tied up with the political power structures or under their control.

Nevertheless, the continued existence of the caliphate had a crucial symbolic importance for the unity and identity of the Muslim world that became increasingly important in the conflict with Western colonialism. A powerful example is the caliphate movement among the Muslim population in India during the struggle for independence in the early decades of the 20th century. The abolition of the caliphate by Turkey thus led to a crisis of identity within the Muslim community. The Turkish decision revealed that the political order in the Islamic world had been based on a set of myths and idealizations that in the conflict-laden encounters with the West had proved no longer to be tenable. In the first decade of the 20th century there had already been a constitutional revolution against the authoritarian regime of the Shah, which, although unable to achieve its aim of instituting a constitution based on Western civic principles, nevertheless paved the way toward a new political order in the Islamic countries. From 1925 until the Islamic revolution of 1979, the Pahlavi rulers in Iran continued the transformation of the legal and economic order based on Western models. Under the determined leadership of Mustafa Kemal, Turkey also followed this path by establishing a secular republic based on Western principles in which the legal order of *sharia* was superseded by a Swiss-inspired civil code, and religious institutions subjected to state control. With the end of the British and French protectorates and colonial rule and the formation of nation-states in Indonesia, Pakistan, Egypt, and the Arab countries, a secular model of political order prevailed in the Muslim world, even if most countries maintained a basically religious orientation rather than the secularism of Turkey.

Abul ala Mawdudi (1903–1979) and the movement he founded, *Jamaat-i-Islami*, advocated the Islamic tradition of an order based on *sharia*, as a result of debate among Indian Muslims. He was critical of the proposal to found a Muslim nation-state in Pakistan, considering it an abuse of universalist Islam to use it as the basis for the formation of a nation-state. He was primarily interested in a revolution in consciousness, in order to promote the renewal of Islamic values as the necessary precondition of founding an Islamic state. Such a state could be established only on the basis of submitting to the authority and absolute sovereignty of God and recognizing *sharia* as an expression of an autonomous order of life and an all-encompassing social order. However, his proposals for an Islamic constitution were unsuccessfully politically. Nevertheless, although his *Jamaat-i-Islami* movement remained in the opposition in Pakistan, this did not diminish its more far-reaching influence on the movements of political Islam.

This is especially true for developments in Egypt. In 1922 and 1923, Rashid Rida had already taken part in the discussion about the caliphate. After a detailed study of the historical origins and the religious and political functions of the caliphate and its subsequent debasement, he concluded that a restoration of the caliphate could be conceived, at best, as being a purely religious office without any political rights. This would not, of course, resolve the problem of an autonomous political reform in the spirit of Islam, and Rida turned to the idea of an Islamic state, basing himself on the ideas of his teacher, Abduh, and picking up the proposal of Mawdudi. He was critical of the principle of sovereignty of the people, advocated by supporters of a secular order and their defense of lawmaking as a political task. Instead, he advocated an Islamic understanding of democracy, based on the principle of *sharia*, as a consultation between rulers and ruled. Legal scholars were traditionally the appointed representatives of the people vis-à-vis the government and thus Rida, like Abduh before him, advocated restoring the independence of the *ulama* from the structures of political power. He also adopted Abduh's distinction between the immutable norms of *sharia* as religious duties established by divine revelation, on the one hand, and the regulation of social relationships on the other, which needed to be adapted to the prevailing social conditions and were therefore the result of human, political jurisprudence. Such jurisprudence, however, needed to hold to the principles of *sharia* and the practice of *ijtihad*. Although the supreme authority in such an Islamic state could be in the hands of a caliph or imam, they would, however, have no direct political role, but instead ensure compliance with the principles of *sharia*. Such a conception of an Islamic state thus has little in common with the image of a system that holds absolute power over all areas of social, political, and cultural life. Rida maintained the distinction between the political and the religious order as it had developed in the Islamic tradition. The ambiguity of the project of an Islamic state was the starting point for the Islamist movement with its clear subordination of politics to religious principles and the use of religious tradition as a means of political mobilization.

The development of Islamism is tied up with the founding of the Muslim Brotherhood in 1928 by Hasan al-Banna (1906–1949).[8] The son of a local imam in Egypt, Banna came into touch with the ideas and writings of Abduh and Rida in the course of his training as a teacher. He wanted to help the younger generation rediscover a genuine understanding of Islam and to reduce the harmful influences of the Western, secular culture of the intellectual elite in Egypt. This was his aim in founding the Muslim Brotherhood, which initially focused on activities of education, public education, and social work. The beginnings of the conflict between the Zionists in Israel and the Arabs in the 1930s led to the initial radicalization of the movement. In 1939 Banna turned the Muslim Brotherhood, which by then had 50,000 members, into a political organization with Islam as its ideological foundation. He believed that Islam was a self-contained system, based on the Qu'ran and the Sunnah, and applicable in all places and at all times. The programme of the organization now aimed at liberating not only Egypt but the whole of the Muslim world from foreign control, with the obligation of establishing a free Islamic government for the Muslim community, based on the principles of Islam and which would be applied to society as a whole. All Muslims would be guilty of an offense against God as long as such an Islamic state had not been established. The United Nations partition plan adopted in 1947 for Israel-Palestine and the subsequent Arab-Israeli war further radicalized the movement, which now did not shrink from violence. In the wake of internal unrest in Egypt, the Brotherhood was disbanded in 1948. Banna himself was assassinated in 1949.

After Banna's death, the moderate wing of the Brotherhood attempted to achieve political rehabilitation, while the radical wing converged with the Movement of Free Officers. The successful military coup against the monarchy in 1952 seemed to bring the ideals of the Brotherhood within reach. However, after an assassination attempt by a militant member of the Brotherhood against General Nasser, who advocated Arab socialism on a nonreligious basis, the organization was again dissolved. Many of its leaders went into exile in Saudi Arabia, were executed, or sentenced to long prison terms, including Banna's successor Sayyid Qutb (1906–1966). Qutb, an Egyptian journalist, had already become the theoretician of the Brotherhood during Banna's lifetime. Originally more pro-Western, he was shocked by his experience of Western freedom during a trip to the United States in 1948, and believed the roots of this situation lay in the separation of religion from the life of society. This strengthened his belief that a viable social order could be developed only on the basis of Islam. The members of the Brotherhood who fled to Saudi Arabia came into closer contact there with local Wahhabi fundamentalism. This was reflected in Qutb's writings, which he composed during his imprisonment. He asserted that Islamic societies may also exist in a state of pre-Islamic "ignorance" (*jahiliyyah*), against which the prophet Muhammad proceeded with unrelenting harshness. This term was originally used about the desert tribes of the Arabian Peninsula and Qutb now applied it to the Islamic societies of his own time. He proclaimed the legitimacy of the jihad against the ruling elites of these societies, who had now become, alongside the "far" enemy of the Western imperialist powers, the "near" enemy that needed to be defeated. His goal was to establish an Islamic state; an order that corresponded to the absolute authority and sovereignty of God needed to be set against the state of "ignorance" in which the rule and sovereignty is exercised by the people. This central idea of the rule of God (*Allah hakimiyyat*) needed to be embodied in the application of Islamic law and the implementation of an Islamic way of life. After a long stretch in prison, Qutb was executed in 1966.

After Anwar al-Sadat succeeded Nasser in 1970 as president of Egypt, the moderate wing of the Brotherhood shifted toward a policy of compromise with the government. In the new constitution of 1971, Islam once again became the state religion and Sadat tolerated the Brotherhood, without legalizing them. The moderate members of the Brotherhood gained in support and prestige, and set about influencing the institutions of the state as a political group. The radical branch split into two groups: the "community of Jihad" and the "community of Islam." From their ranks came the assassins who assassinated Sadat during a military parade in 1981. It was through the Egyptian doctor Ayman al-Zawahiri, who belonged to the radical circles linked to the Muslim Brotherhood, and who became an extreme Islamist prepared to engaged in violence during his imprisonment after the death of Sadat, that contacts developed during the war in Afghanistan to Osama bin-Laden and thus to the terrorist Islamism of al-Qaeda.⁹ Al-Zawahiri was named leader of al-Qaeda after the death of bin-Laden in 2011.

The influence of violent political Islam as represented by the Islamism of the Muslim Brotherhood, in which Islam has become a political ideology to combat the ruling elites as representatives of a secular, Western-oriented model, and in general to oppose the domination of the Muslim world by the West, represented in particular by the role of Israel in the Middle East, extended far beyond Egypt. Clear examples are the Palestinian Hamas movement, which is directly inspired by the ideology of the Muslim Brotherhood, and similar movements in North Africa and Southeast Asia. A characteristic feature of them all is that their leaders, like many of their members, come from the new urban middle class that has benefited from modern education. In contrast to the reformists already mentioned, they are less interested in questions of the interpretation of Islamic tradition than in an alternative social order in which Islamic identity develops through a process of conflict with Western modernity. With their revolutionary ideology, they are reacting both to the experience of humiliation and a feeling of inferiority toward the seemingly all-powerful West, and a widespread disillusionment following the dashed expectations and unfulfilled promises of modernization programmes in the Arab states. The political project of establishing an Islamic state where *sharia* determines the social and political order is the expression of an idealized image of early Islam that is at odds with the realities of Islamic history but that is now used as a utopia to mobilize in political struggle. As the overview above of the reform discussion demonstrated, there is as yet no binding understanding of an Islamic political order, nor an authoritative interpretation of *sharia*. In particular, bringing the obligations of religious (and legal) traditions of Islam into accordance with the requirements of viable state structures is still the subject of heated debate in the Muslim community. Nowhere has the revolutionary ideology of Islamism managed to establish itself politically on a lasting basis.

Even the term "Islamic state" is used quite liberally and indiscriminately. It can refer to all states in which Islam is the majority or state religion, or simply to all the members of the Organization of Islamic Conference. However, they differ greatly from each other in their form of government and their legal systems. There is not yet a single understanding of how the principles of *sharia* law can be brought into line with a constitutional order appropriate to contemporary global needs. Only two states may lay claim to meet the strict sense of what it means to be an Islamic state, namely Saudi Arabia and the Islamic Republic of Iran. The Islamic Republic of Sudan might also be counted among them, with certain qualifications. Saudi Arabia is an absolute monarchy, in which, as already mentioned, not only has Islam been declared the sole official religion, but the Qur'an and the Sunnah of the Prophet have been given constitutional status. Despite recent missionary efforts emanating from Saudi Arabia, the rigorous Wahhabi Islam found there enjoys no support among the vast majority of Sunni Muslims and their governments. Neither can the Iranian model be applied elsewhere. It is rooted in the features of the Shiite tradition to which we have already made brief reference. On the one hand, there is the higher authority of the legal scholar, who as the representative (*Statthalter*) of the imam has a religiously based claim to leadership vis-à-vis all forms of political governance. Then there is the traditional practice of rational interpretation (*ijtihad*) of the *sharia* and the strict distinction between obligatory religious duties and the particular requirements of social order and conditions, and finally the martyr cult of Husayn and an apocalyptic tendency linked to the expectation of the return of the Hidden Imam. Even the "theocracy" of Iran, a political system in which the guardians of the religious tradition of Shiite Islam are accorded supreme authority for political decisions, are confronted by the expectations and confidence of a growing, modern educated population, especially among the younger generation. In Sudan, finally, Islam is the state religion, but following the peace agreement of 2005, which led to the independence of South Sudan in 2011, *sharia* as the basis of legislation was restricted to the northern, predominantly Muslim part of the country, though it is unclear how this applies to non-Muslim minorities.

ISLAMIC PERSPECTIVES FOR A NEW WORLD ORDER

Islamism, particularly in its violent form, is only one of the political expressions of Islam that has developed in the second half of the 20th century, albeit one that is widespread and that has gained international attention. Political Islam is an expression of the inner struggle within Islamic societies for self-determination and for the recovery of an Islamic identity following the period of colonization and the subsequent separation of the Muslim community into nation-states with precarious legitimacy. The emergence of political Islam is a result of a conscious revival of Islamic traditions and values, and reflects ambivalence about the process of modernization, since political Islam also uses the methods and instruments of Western-style modernity.

Urbanization, and the associated development of modern forms of communication, transport, and particularly mass media, have thus been essential preconditions for the emergence of political Islam.[10] Another factor is the greatly expanded access to education, ranging from elementary literacy programmes among the rural population to high-quality training for highly specialized professions in the modern sector of social and economic life. An articulate public has been created in Islamic countries through newspapers, magazines, books and electronic means of communication, which have taken on a vitality of their own through the use made of them by a variety of social and religious groups and associations. Most of the initiatives and movements of political Islam have their origins in this environment of an emerging civil society and are thus part of this process of modernization.

The process of globalization has both reinforced and accentuated this trend. On the one hand, economic globalization has led to the growing interdependence of Islamic countries with the world economy and to the emergence of an Islamic diaspora in many Western countries and elsewhere. At the same time, modern transportation allows increasing numbers of Muslims to fulfil their religious duty of pilgrimage to Mecca, thus giving them a direct experience of the universal and global character of Islam. On the other hand, the impact of cultural globalization in Muslim societies has reinforced efforts to strengthen their distinctive, religiously based identity and thus to underline their independence in the world of nations. The Organization of the Islamic Conference (OIC) founded in 1969 may thus also be seen as an expression of political Islam in response to globalization.

Of course, there is as yet no clear and definitive answer to the question as to how, in a globalized, ineluctably interdependent world, Islam and state politics can be reconciled, or at least brought into a constructive relationship with each other. At the centre of the vigorous debate between the extremes of Islamists on the one hand and secularists on the other, with reformists and traditionalists somewhere in the middle, is the question of which of the historical forms of Islamic tradition on the relationship between religion and politics is seen as binding and whether the use of independent judgment (*ijtihad*) is legitimate in the interpretation and development of tradition.[11] Secularists follow the example of Kemalist Turkey in advocating the strict separation of religion and politics and the banishment of religion from the public space. For a time, such a position of strict secularism was linked with socialist options in state politics, thus strongly underlining social justice and the common good in the tradition of the Qu'ran, but this has now lost much of its support in the Muslim world. The main reason has been the steadily increasing influence in recent decades of Islamists, who see the separation of religion and politics as a betrayal of the Islamic tradition and as a Western strategy to weaken the Islamic community. They advocate the establishment of an Islamic state based on *sharia* and the rigorous subordination of state politics to the sovereignty of God and God's teachings. As shown above, this is an ahistorical, utopian projection of the idealized past of the way in which the Muslim community in Medina first took shape, ignoring all subsequent experience of the relationship and necessary differentiation between the specific roles of religious institutions and state politics. The Islamist position has thus far failed the reality check, but there are signs of a growing willingness even among some Islamists, such as those in Egypt and Algeria, to participate constructively and cooperatively in the political process.

The two remaining options—those of the traditionalists and the reformers caught in the middle—were for a long time overshadowed by the violent, ideological struggle for power between Islamists and the secular ruling elites. The traditionalists, represented by the institutions of religious and legal scholars, have lost much of their authority because of their close association to the structures of power and by their insistence on using the received rules of interpreting Islamic tradition. They lack the sophisticated knowledge of the modern social and political context. They also see themselves as lacking the authority to return to the practice of independent judgment (*ijtihad*) and in many cases are unable to offer answers to the pressing challenges facing Islamic societies. The reformers, by contrast, can look back to an impressive pedigree in the discourse on reform, but for a long time were forced onto the defensive both by the Islamists and by the traditionalists, thus being obliged to demonstrate their belief in law and Islamic legitimacy. Their voice is now being heard more clearly by the Islamic public. This is because, on the one hand, of the apparent lack of legitimacy of state structures in the eyes of the majority in most Muslim countries, and thus the limited capacity of governments to act within the international sphere, and, on the other, by the loss of credibility of the radical, Islamist option because of its association with international terrorism, which has discredited Islam as a whole and, in the global context, made it an enemy image.

As far as Islamic perspectives for a new world order and for the redefinition of the relationship between religion and politics in Islam are concerned, the important issues include: openness to democratic political structures; the recognition of equal dignity, rights, and obligations for all people and nations; a commitment to dialogue and peaceful cooperation; a endorsement of the criteria of social and economic justice; and the application of a critical hermeneutic in interpreting the Islamic legal tradition. The strength of the reform discourse is that it tackles the internal problems of Islamic societies, especially the lack of public, democratic participation in the political process, which could lend new legitimacy to state structures. Compared to the Islamist option for which the source of legitimacy is found only in exclusivist interpretations of religious traditions, thus appearing confrontational and potentially totalitarian to other systems and those with a different way of thinking, the reform discourse is based on the principle enshrined in Islamic tradition of open consultation and the search for consensus in the Muslim community, which does not exclude dissident positions but integrates them.

The reformers are also concerned about preserving and affirming Islamic identity rather than simply adapting to the standards of political order that come from outside. They insist, however, that there has never in Islamic history been a single dimension of Islamic identity binding on all Muslims, and that demands for the recognition of the principle of self-determination of Muslim countries in an international context must be applied equally to internal debate.[12] Referring to the inner meaning of the statements of the Qur'an about the principle of consultation (*shura*) and given the nondemocratic nature of the political structures during most of Islamic history, Kamal Aboulmagd concludes: "The essence of the *Islamicity* of any government is to guarantee the consent of the people as the basis and criterion for the legitimacy of political power and authority."[13]

The discussion on the issue of religious freedom at the end of the previous chapter concluded with a plea for the "public space" to become a place of discourse and communication about the living conditions of the human community and described religious freedom as a fundamental instrument by which this space may be protected. The "Cairo Declaration of Human Rights in Islam" mentioned at the beginning of this chapter states that *sharia* is the sole basis of human rights and thus appears to declare that the principles of Islam are incompatible with religious freedom, as set out in 1948 in Article 18 of the Universal Declaration of Human Rights. Abdullahi A. An-Na'im, a Sudanese-born law professor at Emory University in Atlanta, Georgia, and an internationally recognized expert in the field of human rights in Islam and from an intercultural perspective, summarizes the traditional statements of *sharia* to religious rights as follows:

> ... a person is essentially "free" to adopt or reject Islam, but certain consequences will follow from his/her choice.
>
> (1) If a person chooses to become a Muslim, or is born and raised as a Muslim, then he or she will have full rights of citizenship in an Islamic state, subject to limitations against the rights of women as conceived in modern constitutional and human rights law. However, once a Muslim or officially classified as such, a person will be subject to the death penalty if he or she becomes an apostate, that is, one who persists in repudiating his or her faith in Islam. An apostate is also subjected to forfeiture of property, nullification of marriage, and other legal consequences.
>
> (2) If a person chooses to be or remain a Christian, Jew, or believer in another scriptural religion, as defined by Shari'a—one of *ahl al-kitab*, the People of the Book or believers in divine scripture who are called *dhimmis*—he or she will suffer certain limitations of rights as a subject of an Islamic state. There are differences in the scope and extent of these limitations among various schools of thought and individual scholars of Shari'a and the practice has also varied over time. The essential point is that *dhimmis* are not supposed to enjoy complete legal equality with Muslims.
>
> (3) If a person is neither a Muslim nor one of *ahl al-kitab*, as defined by Shari'a, then that person is deemed to be an unbeliever (*khafir* or *mushrik*). An unbeliever is not permitted to reside

permanently, or even temporarily according to stricter interpretations, in peace as a free person within the territory of an Islamic state except under special permission for safe conduct (*aman*). In theory, unbelievers should be offered the choice of adopting Islam, and if they reject it they may either be killed in battle, enslaved, or ransomed if captured.[14]

Apart from this, Muslims are not permitted to reside permanently in a non-Muslim state.

This system of religious rights, at the time it was drawn up, was probably superior to the situation in other countries or empires with a "state religion." Moreover, the principles have been generally interpreted in terms of allowing greater religious freedom. They assume, however, an identity of nationality and religion, which prevailed even in Europe until the 19th century, but is incompatible with contemporary understandings of the equality of fundamental civic rights irrespective of race, class, culture, gender, and religious affiliation. Tying the understanding of human rights and religious freedom to the traditionalist interpretation of *sharia* would oblige Muslims to chose between Islam and *sharia* on the one hand, and democracy and human rights on the other, between "secular" individualism or "Islamic" communitarianism. The reform discourse opposes such coercion.[15]

It therefore actively advocates the application of a critical hermeneutic as understood by *ijtihad* in the interpretation of *sharia*. This interpretation is based on the following conditions:

> First, since Shari'a is a historically-conditioned human interpretation of the fundamental sources of Islam, alternative modern interpretations are possible. Second, a reconstruction of Shari'a in support of Islamic foundations for religious human rights is imperative in view of the need for contesting and renegotiating Islamic identity and its normative system in the present circumstances of plurality of national and international political communities. Third, such a theory will be fully Islamic, because

it would be based on the text of the Qur'an as interpreted and accepted by Muslims in the present context, instead of applying Shari'a principles which were the product of interpretation by earlier Muslims in their own historical context.[16]

This is exemplified by the death penalty pronounced in *sharia* for apostasy, which dates back to early reports from the Sunnah. It may be explained, among other reasons, as an expression of a social order in which infidelity was considered high treason because nationality and citizenship were based on belief in Islam. Today, however, most Muslims live in multireligious nation-states that are involved in global interaction and which are continually exposed to cultural and social interaction with non-Islamic states.[17] Given these changed circumstances, a new interpretation of the sources of Islam is required. The new framework for interpretation is neither arbitrary nor relativistic, because the credibility of the proposed interpretation depends on the judgment of a living community exercised in serious public discussion and debate.

On the issue of the legitimacy of the political order, the reform discourse needs to deal with Islamic fundamentalism, and on the issue of religious freedom, it needs to deal with the traditionalist interpretation of *sharia*. When it comes to the relationship between religion and politics, the reform discourse is confronted with the position of the secularists, who advocate the fundamental constitutional separation of religion and politics. This option may have some utility in countering Islamist demands for an Islamic state governed by *sharia*. It fails to recognize, however, the fundamental importance of Islam for the collective and individual identity of the people in Islamic countries. Attempts to enforce political secularism would meet insurmountable resistance, as demonstrated by recent history. Instead of Islamic societies having to make a radical choice between the complete unity or the complete separation of Islam and state politics, the reform discourse attempts to deal with and to redefine the relationship between religion and politics, based on an awareness of Islamic identity and the urge of self-determination, without coming into conflict with internationally recognized standards of human rights.[18] Such redefinition is based on the understanding that the Western forms of the principle of separation of religion and politics, or of church and state, were the result of a process of secularization that developed under specific historical conditions, and that cannot and should not simply be applied to other social and cultural contexts. From the Muslim perspective, moreover, the secular option is burdened by its connection with Western colonialism and postcolonial hegemonic claims.

The relationship between the principles of the Muslim tradition and contemporary requirements for the structures of political authority therefore needs further clarification. It is thus important to create space for public debate, through which the results of scientific research that seeks to distinguish between fundamental Islamic values and the earlier situation of Muslim societies can be absorbed and appreciated. "From this perspective, the protection of basic human rights, especially freedom of belief, expression, and association, is an Islamic imperative—and merely a requirement of international treaties—because these rights are prerequisites for the necessary discourse."[19]

Future Perspectives

Such questions have been discussed intensively in recent decades in the context of interreligious dialogue, especially between Muslim and Christian representatives. These opportunities for dialogue have, in their own way, helped to expand the space for public debate, even and especially in the Muslim world. A brief look at key findings and declarations, especially of meetings for Christian-Muslim dialogue, therefore concludes this chapter.

Since 1991, the World Council of Churches has conducted a series of consultations and meetings with Muslim religious leaders. Reference has already been made several times to the reports of the consultations from 1992 to 1994 on issues of "Religion, Law and Society."[20] The focus of these discussions was the place of religion in state and society, the interpretation of *sharia*, the understanding of secularism, the relationship between religion and nationality, and especially the importance of human rights in a religiously plural world. The report of the consultation of 1994 notes here:

> Already, we were able together to affirm principles of common citizenship and religious liberty, respect for freedom of conscience, dignity of the person, the equal status of women, sanctity of the family, equality of opportunity, respect for property, and belief in the integrity of creation. While we considered these principles universally applicable, we also recognized that their practical expression will vary from time to time and place to place in respect for particular religious and cultural traditions, without compromising their essence.[21]

At the end of 2000, another meeting of Christian and Muslim representatives took stock of the experiences of dialogue since 1991.[22] The subsequent report states:

> In a context where religions are finding renewed public vigour, issues of freedom of conscience and human rights generally have re-emerged, in the last few years, as sensitive and even divisive. In this respect, Christian-Muslim dialogue has an indispensable contribution to make in affirming that the principles of human rights and religious freedom are indivisible. . . . Muslims and Christians agree that freedom of conscience is essential to their respective faiths. But religious freedom does not only imply freedom of conscience but also the right to live in accord with religious values and the recognition of cultural and religious diversity as basic to human reality. More broadly, Christians and Muslims can contribute, through dialogue, to a discourse on human rights that can help reconcile the truly universal principles and the culturally specific claims.

> Religious affiliations that unite people with others beyond their national borders need not contradict equal citizenship. Multiple identities are a fact of human existence.... In dialogue, no dimension of personal identity excludes another. The more dialogue partners feel secure in their own identities, the more they are able to be inclusive and engage in wider interreligious and intercultural relations and interaction.[23]

In October 2002, thus after the attacks of 11 September 2001, the WCC held an international consultation with senior representatives of key Muslim and Christian organizations on the theme "Christians and Muslims in Dialogue and Beyond."[24] The report of the consultation states:

> Our Muslim and Christian beliefs lead us to share a common understanding of the dignity of the human being and on that foundation we together affirm the fundamental rights of individuals and groups as expressed in the UN Declaration of Human Rights and the reciprocal duties which flow from those rights. We assert that all, regardless of religion, race, ethnicity, gender or class, are entitled to full and equal citizenship rights and freedom of expression and religion in whatever country they may belong to. We especially confirm that the equal participation of religions and religious communities in public affairs locally, nationally and internationally is not only a right but also a duty which flows directly from our commitment as people who believe that our scriptures and core teachings have an essential message to society today. It follows that we also affirm the freedom of the individual to adhere to the religion of his or her choice, and that it is the function of the state to protect the full and equal right of all religious communities to organise themselves and to participate appropriately in public affairs.[25]

The Roman Catholic Church has also engaged in intensive dialogue with Islam. These efforts were given a special urgency and importance after the Regensburg speech of Pope Benedict XVI in

September 2006 and the debate it triggered.[26] The following year (October 2007) 138 Muslim religious scholars published an open letter to Pope Benedict XVI and senior representatives of Christian churches and denominations with a call for peace and cooperation, "A Common Word between Us and You."[27] This states:

> Muslims and Christians together make up well over half of the world's population. Without peace and justice between these two religious communities, there can be no meaningful peace in the world. The future of the world depends on peace between Muslims and Christians. The basis for this peace and understanding already exists. It is part of the very foundational principles of both faiths: love of the One God, and love of the neighbour. These principles are found over and over again in the sacred texts of Islam and Christianity. The Unity of God, the necessity of love for Him, and the necessity of love of the neighbour is thus the common ground between Islam and Christianity.[28]

In March 2008, the theological dialogue was institutionalized through the establishment of the "Catholic-Muslim Forum." In June of the same year, the League of the Islamic World took the initiative to organize the International Islamic Conference for Dialogue, which brought senior Sunni and Shiite religious leaders together in Mecca. The focus of the "Mecca Declaration" elaborated at the meeting is, according to Udo Steinbach,

> that the appeal for dialogue between revealed religions has been willed by God himself through the diversity of religions. It was clear that this appeal was no easy task for the theologians gathered in Mecca, since it implies renouncing the claim that Islam contains the only genuine revelation of the one God. With their appeal to the civilizations, cultures and philosophies, academics, media and religious leaders, they are acknowledging that Islam, Christianity and Judaism are on the same level as far as their religious substance is concerned.[29]

The next month, in July 2008, the Muslim World League hosted a world conference on dialogue in Madrid. The "Declaration of Madrid" agreed by 300 representatives from the religions and civilizations who gathered there formulated ten fundamental principles for dialogue.[30] In addition to affirming the unity of humanity and the equality of all people regardless of race, ethnic background, or culture, the declaration states that "Respecting human dignity, promoting human rights, fostering peace, honouring agreements and respecting the traditions of peoples as well as their right to security, freedom and self-determination, are the basis for building good relations among all peoples."[31]

Against this background, the final declaration of the first meeting of the "Catholic-Muslim Forum," held in November 2008, in Rome, takes on a particular significance. The debate focused on two broad themes: "Theological and Spiritual Foundations" and "Human Dignity and Mutual Respect."[32] Among the 15 points of the declaration, the following are particularly important for the issues discussed in this chapter:

> 3. Human dignity is derived from the fact that every human person is created by a loving God out of love, and has been endowed with the gifts of reason and free will, and therefore enabled to love God and others. On the firm basis of these principles, the person requires the respect of his or her original dignity and his or her human vocation. Therefore, he or she is entitled to full recognition of his or her identity and freedom by individuals, communities and governments, supported by civil legislation that assures equal rights and full citizenship . . .
>
> 5. Genuine love of neighbour implies respect of the person and her or his choices in matters of conscience and religion. It includes the right of individuals and communities to practice their religion in private and public.
>
> 6. Religious minorities are entitled to be respected in their own religious convictions and practices. They are also entitled to

their own places of worship, and their founding figures and symbols they consider sacred should not be subject to any form of mockery or ridicule.

8. We affirm that no religion and its followers should be excluded from society. Each should be able to make its indispensable contribution to the good of society, especially in service to the most needy.

This overview based on a selection of voices from the field of reform discourse and Christian-Muslim dialogue makes clear that there is a lively discussion among Islamic scholars in Islamic societies about the role of religion within the social order. Its progress will be crucial in dealing with the relationship between religion and politics in a new world order. It will be particularly important in this task to strengthen the space of the public sphere of civil society to overcome a state-centred understanding of politics.

4. The Challenge of Fundamentalism

Chapter 2 concluded that we cannot do away with the modern distinction between the two spheres of religion and politics, but that neither should they be seen as being completely separate from each other, for the sake of the transparency and legitimacy of political order and for the credibility and integrity of religion. It became clear from reviewing the various forms of public religion in postcolonial states, and particularly from the more detailed investigation of the relationship between religion and politics in the Muslim world past and present, that the model of the legal and institutional separation of church and state used in the European and American context cannot be applied as such to other situations. Instead, the modalities of the way in which religion and politics are distinguished from, or related to, each other in any given context need to be constantly redefined and renegotiated.

This also applies to the United States of America, the country in which the principle of the separation of religion and politics, or of church and state, was first formulated, and then enforced through an amendment to the Constitution. The brief review of the developments in the United States in chapter 2 demonstrated that this constitutional principle did not aim at removing religion from the public sphere, as it did in France, but rather at founding a functioning public order in which there was no need to suppress the religious dimension of collective identity. While the language of the Declaration of Independence and of the Constitution and its amendments dispensed with any direct religious legitimization, there has been much stronger reference to the religious founding myth of the United States in the way in which collective identity is expressed.

In his analysis of the relationship between religion and politics in the United States, Rainer Prätorius makes a distinction between two forms of religion. "Religion 1" is the "organized religious practice in a specific religious community, such as Baptists, Reform Jews or Buddhists." He distinguishes this from "Religion 2," an understanding of religion that refers to "a general religious attitude, a belief in God, certain timeless principles characteristic of Christianity but not limited to it."[1] Following Tocqueville and Rousseau, Robert Bellah refers to this second understanding of religion as "civil religion," examining its function for the cohesion of society, but also pointing to the danger of the misuse of civil religion by sectional religious interests.

The American form of separation of religion and politics, or church and state, ultimately rests on an implicit distinction between "public" and "private" religion. This distinction is unproblematic as long as there are limits to the range of "private" particular expressions of religion, and all specifically religious communities have a place in the principles and attitudes of the civil religion. This was true for the founding phase of the United States and until the second half of the 19th century. In particular, the great revival movement of the 1830s, linked to the names of Jonathan Edwards (1703–1758) and George Whitefield (1714–1770), made this rather pietistic-evangelical Protestantism the *de facto* public religion of the United States. The Declaration of Independence had indeed referred to a "God of Nature" and the publicly sanctioned symbols and rituals of civil religion avoided any explicit reference to the Christian "God of history." But a defining factor for social and political life was the awareness rooted in the Protestant tradition of "God's Covenant with America" and America's special calling as a "light unto the nations."

The second wave of revivals (c. 1837–1838), primarily linked to the name of the Methodist preacher Charles Finney (1792–1875), was also based on the confidence of the religiously utopian project of building the new Jerusalem. The hegemony of this religiously shaped public culture, which complemented the constitutionally defined framework of the separation of church and state, was maintained until the second half of the 19th century.

The rise of Christian fundamentalism as an idea and as a form of religious (and political) practice cannot be separated from "revivalist" Protestantism gradually losing the self-evident role as a public religion that it had occupied for many generations in the United States. The concept of "fundamentalism" is linked to a theological, ethical, moral, and political attempt to restore the hegemony of a public culture dominated by Protestantism as a bulwark against the cultural, social, and political influences of secular modernity. Fundamentalism is not to be identified simply with an attitude of traditionalism, the insistence on maintaining traditional forms and opposing any kind of change. Fundamentalism is, rather, a conscious response to a breach that has already taken place through which tradition has lost its unquestioned self-evident status. This observation applies to all forms of fundamentalism, as will be shown later in this chapter. The main features of fundamentalist positions will be sketched out by examining the origins of Christian fundamentalism in the United States.

The clearest summary of the fundamentalist position is to be found in the book *Christianity and Liberalism* (1923)[2] by J. Gresham Machen, a New Testament scholar at Princeton Theological Seminary. The customary description of this church and theological standpoint as "fundamentalism" came only around 1920 and referred to the publication of a 12-volume series entitled "The Fundamentals: A Testimony to the Truth" (1910–1915). This series offered an explanation of the fundamental elements of an evangelical understanding of faith, as it is set down and witnessed to in "revivalist"

Protestantism as an all-encompassing truth and worldview. At the same time its distinctive criteria were formulated in the struggle against liberal and modernist positions in theology and church.

Alongside premillenarian eschatology and the strict theological defense of the biblical worldview, the theory of *dispensationalism* was important for the shape of fundamentalism in the first third of the 20th century. This theory was brought into American discussions and debates by the English theologian John Nelson Darby (1800–1882).[3] Dispensationalism is a hermeneutic theory, according to which differences and contradictions within and between the biblical writings are not due to the various human authors, but to different periods of God's saving action. The consequences for biblical interpretation were first demonstrated by Cyrus I. Scofield (1843–1921) in his popular *Scofield Reference Bible*. When linked to premillenarian eschatology, dispensationalism reinforced a belief in Christ's imminent return. On the other hand, according to this doctrine, the return of Christ needs to be preceded by the return of Israel to the promised land and the rebuilding of the Temple in Jerusalem. From this results a complex scenario of the end times in which American policy in relation to Israel plays a key role. At the same time, dispensationalism sets out an expectation, referring to 1 Thessalonians 4:16ff., that before the great tribulation preceding the return of Christ, believers will be "caught up" to enter the millennial kingdom with Christ.

The early champions of fundamentalism were unable to achieve their goal of theologically refuting the liberal position and driving it out of the church. On the contrary, this attempt ended with the retreat of the fundamentalist groups into a sect-like existence. Even the cultural and political struggle to reaffirm American self-understanding as a "Christian nation" came to nothing. In the field of culture, fundamentalists attempted to preserve the prevailing Christian influence on education and moral instruction. Here the conflict concentrated on rebutting Darwin's theory of evolution, on the one hand, and, on prohibition, the proscription of the sale of alcohol, on the other. In some states, including Tennessee, they managed to achieve a statutory prohibition on the teaching of evolution being included in school lessons. When this prohibition was challenged in a spectacular court case in Dayton in 1925, the fundamentalist position was confirmed by the court, but it lost any remaining significant support from the wider public. The court case marked the end of the first phase of fundamentalism.

This early fundamentalism left no lasting traces as far as the relationship between religion and politics in the United States was concerned. Instead of the pugnacious and confrontational approach of fundamentalism, the integrative capacity of the dominant form of Protestantism, which gathered both liberal and moderate evangelical elements, was further strengthened. It continued to function as the framework of "public religion," thus confirming again the particular balance between religion and politics that, despite the constitutional separation, had taken shape in the United States.

The Political Shift of Fundamentalism

There was a marked revival of traditional evangelicalism during the administration of President Dwight D. Eisenhower (1953–1961), linked to the name of evangelist Billy Graham. He would become a privileged interlocutor and pastor for several presidents.[4] At the same time charismatic and Pentecostal denominations gained in influence, especially through the use of television as a means of evangelism.

Despite the reaffirmation of the traditional profile of "Christian America," this period was also marked by renewed uncertainty about American identity. This was linked to the conflicts unleashed by the civil rights movement and the legislation introduced under the Johnson administration, student unrest and opposition to the Vietnam War, the assassinations of John F. Kennedy, Martin Luther King Jr., and Robert Kennedy, and the forced resignation of President Nixon as a result of the Watergate scandal. The guardians of conservative ideas of Christian morality saw the Supreme Court decision to allow abortion (1973) as a clear attack on the Christian tradition. This is the context in which fundamentalist positions with a clear political profile experienced a revival.

This second fundamentalist wave in the United States is linked to the emergence of the "New Christian Right" on the public, political stage.[5] The central figure in the early phase of this movement was the founder of the so-called Moral Majority, Jerry Falwell, a successful televangelist and president of Liberty University, which has a conservative evangelical orientation. The founding of the Moral Majority in 1979 was the result of a deliberate political coalition between neo-conservative Republicans such as Paul Weyrich, Gary Bauer, and Ralph Reed, and representatives of conservative religious groups, like Falwell and Pat Robertson. The background to this was the frustration of conservative political groups over their loss of power after President Nixon's resignation and the disappointment of conservative evangelicals that the first avowed evangelical president, Jimmy Carter, had not promoted a conservative political agenda.

Founded as a movement that transcended religion, the Moral Majority aimed at political involvement based around common conservative values, that is, "pro-life, pro-family, pro-traditional moral (sic), pro-America and pro-Israel."[6] This required the conservative evangelical sector, now accounting for a quarter of the U.S. population, and the strongest group among Protestants, to be mobilized politically and to take part in elections. Falwell had originally promoted the defensive evangelical position of biblically based abstinence from political involvement. In the course of the developments in the 1970s described above, especially the Supreme Court abortion decision, he came to the conclusion that the "sovereignty" of the conservative lifeworld oriented around the family, the church, and traditional morality was threatened and that an assertive strategy was now needed.[7] At any rate, it was necessary to do all that was possible to realign the traditional "American way of life" with this conservative evangelical strategy.

The Moral Majority's immediate political objective was to mobilize conservative evangelical voters for the 1980 election of Ronald

Reagan as president. The campaign successfully used modern communication technologies and professional methods of fundraising. The religious factor in the electoral behaviour of U.S. voters has steadily increased since Ronald Reagan was first elected. Jerry Falwell withdrew from direct political involvement in the mid-1980s and the Moral Majority disbanded. In its place the "Christian Coalition" came into being in 1988 with the main objective of supporting Pat Robertson's candidacy for the Republican presidential nomination. The results were rather disappointing, and were so again in the elections that followed in 1992 and 1996. The limits of a political strategy based explicitly on religion and morality thus became clear. Even if increasing support from conservative Christian voters for the Republican Party remained extremely important, they could not simply be made into an instrument for the sectional interests of a minority of the American population. The election of George W. Bush in 2000 and his reelection in 2004 was certainly a late success for the strategy of the "New Christian Right" with its stress on the political significance of religious and moral values. In his political rhetoric, President Bush echoed many fundamentalist themes. In practice, however, he was obliged to act more pragmatically in order not to lose electors from the political centre.[8] Barack Obama's overwhelming electoral majority in both 2008 and 2012 appears, however, to mark the end for the moment of the political ambitions of this second form of Christian Protestant fundamentalism.

Fundamentalism as a General Type of Political Religion

So far our observations and analysis have concentrated on the Protestant form of Christian fundamentalism, and particularly its genesis and development in the United States. Such a historical approach seems meaningful, as the term from its very origins has been linked with this specific form of religion. In the meantime, however, the use of the term has been separated from this background and is today used to describe a general type of political religion, or used more widely to denote the militant promotion of political convictions having an absolute status. It is therefore necessary for what follows to define more precisely what it means to talk about the challenge of "fundamentalism."

Fundamentalism is often associated with the aggressive promotion of what is claimed to be an absolute and unchangeable truth, that is, a religious message revealed in Holy Scripture or sacred writings and its binding application for the faith, morals, and life of a community. Behind this are the so-called religions of the book of Judaism, Christianity, and Islam. It is already clear, however, from the analysis of the internal debates in the Muslim world and especially the complex relations between conservative evangelicals and fundamentalists in the United States, that conservative traditionalism, holding fast to a belief in timeless truth of Holy Scripture in the face of a historical critical approach, does not necessarily become fundamentalism in the sense of mounting an aggressive strategy. It is not enough simply to describe religious fundamentalism as "oppositionalism," as an expression of the readiness of traditionalists to defend themselves aggressively against threats to the fundamentals of their religious identity.[9]

At the beginning of this chapter, fundamentalism, in contrast to traditionalism, was described as the "theological, ethical, moral, and political attempt to restore the hegemony of a public culture dominated by Protestantism as a bulwark against the cultural, social and political influences of secular modernity. Fundamentalism is ... [in contrast to traditionalism] ... rather, a conscious response to a breach that has already taken place through which tradition has lost its unquestioned self-evident status."[10] A more general definition by John Coleman from within the sociology of religion notes that fundamentalism raises the threatened or lost autonomy of a sacred tradition to the status of a programme/manifesto:

> Fundamentalists call the people to return to a lost tradition. They call for the reclaiming of the values of a more pristine, allegedly

more integral, era. They seek thereby to reorient society and culture towards a more desirable future. The reconstructed earlier era may, of course, be highly idealized or depend on a very innovative overemphasis on one or other trait of the imagined earlier era.... Importantly, fundamentalism is a modern phenomenon.... Unlike world-rejecting sects and cults, fundamentalists seek to live in modernity (and influence its direction) but not be part of it.... Thus, fundamentalists, typically, do not see themselves as simply reactionary. Rather, they refuse to acquiesce in the inevitability of change, a refusal which expresses a will to shape the world in a way that is different from modern forces. It is this active will to shape a different world that distinguishes fundamentalism from mere traditionalism.[11]

This observation applies to all forms of fundamentalism, as will be shown later in this chapter.

The definition that Heinrich Schäfer proposes at the beginning of his book *Clash of Fundamentalisms*, resulting from his long preoccupation with the phenomenon of fundamentalism, goes in the same direction: "Unlike many other researchers, I propose a strictly formal definition of fundamentalism: movements are fundamentalist if they (1) declare religious convictions (of whatever faith content) as absolute values and (2) derive from this a strategy for the domination of society in which private and public life is subject to the dictates of their religious convictions. The context (3) for such a strategy is the underlying politicisation of all aspects of life through the process of modernization."[12]

The three criteria Schäfer mentions here are closely linked and build on each other. They cover historic Protestant fundamentalism as much as the charismatic, Pentecostal form. The formal definition can also be applied to similar phenomena in other religious and philosophical traditions and lends itself to an analysis of fundamentalism as a general type of political religion. The basis of the definition is the absolutization of convictions and thereby an exclusive understanding of one's own identity, which sets itself apart fundamentally from other ways of interpreting a given tradition. The second criterion marks the difference between resolute, but defensive, traditionalism on the one hand, which restricts itself to the preservation and protection of the sacred tradition, without seeking confrontation with the "heretical" elements of one's own tradition, and fundamentalism in the narrower sense, which seeks to make one's own definition of identity the general rule and thus to impose on the community as a whole through militant confrontation its own absolute differentiation between truth and falsehood, good and evil: "There are in the one and the same religious movement tendencies to retreat into enclaves, and others that pursue aggressive political and economic strategies of power. Both hold their religious beliefs absolutely, the first as protection, the second to gain power."[13]

The third criterion locates fundamentalism in a specific sociopolitical environment, namely the conflicts and upheavals associated with the processes of modernization. Fundamentalism is, as Coleman has also pointed out, a product of modernity. Fundamentalists are responding to the dissolution of a religiously sanctioned order previously taken for granted. They utilize the intentional reconstruction of this order as an ideology in the struggle for decisive influence on the shaping of society in a conflict over modernization. "The battlefield of the fundamentalists are the conflicts over *modern life itself*, and they organize themselves in a highly modern fashion: they are organized as social movements."[14] They take advantage of a situation whereby, with the dissolution of the traditional order, the shaping of social and community life is a question of public and private bargaining between different interests. Fundamentalists intervene in this process by exacerbating a conflict of interests and declaring it to be a conflict about individual and more particularly collective identity. Religiously motivated or legitimized identity politics have thereby become a characteristic feature of fundamentalist movements.

The definitions of Coleman and Schäfer are helpful for the purposes of this study, which aims at clarifying the relationship between religion and politics. They locate fundamentalism in a specific context of conflict, where the relationship between religion and politics comes under pressure from the process of modernization and must be renegotiated. Fundamentalism is both a religious and a political project. It represents a particular type of public, political religion and seeks to guide and dominate public opinion in the public space that has developed as a consequence of social modernization. It involves the deliberate use of modern means of communication, of influencing public opinion and of acquiring power. Fundamentalist strategies aim at transcending the specifically modern forms of distinguishing religion and politics, and differentiating morality and legality, or turning back to a more original unity between these spheres, and thus (re)creating an earlier religiously sanctioned order. Fundamentalism uses the symbolic power of religion to strengthen the awareness of a collective identity, having a tendency to label those with different or opposed views not simply as opponents but as enemies. Fundamentalism is not necessarily violent, but can be used to legitimize a holy war or crusade through a specifically religious (especially eschatological and apocalyptic) view of the world, in which the power of God is in conflict with demonic powers.

Fundamentalist Movements in World Religions

Taking these definitions of fundamentalism as a basis, it is clear that this form of public, political religion is not limited to the form it takes in the conservative evangelical Protestantism of the American tradition. The location of fundamentalism in the specific context of conflicts linked to modernization and the need for the redefinition of collective identity in this tension between religion and politics makes clear that there is a tendency toward the formation of fundamentalist movements in all religions that traditionally have exercised a determining influence on the culture and the order of a particular community. The previous chapters have already pointed to examples of such movements, without explicitly describing them as "fundamentalist."

This is clearly the case for the Islamist movement in the form of the Muslim Brotherhood, and especially in Sayyid Qutb's ideological and political aggrandizement of their objectives. He used the concept of "ignorance" (*jahiliyya*), developed in the early days of building up the Muslim community in the fight against hostile desert tribes, to justify the violent struggle (*jihad*) against the ruling elites in Islamic states. It was necessary to overcome a state of ignorance through the establishment of an Islamic state, in which with the enforcement of Islamic law and the absolute sovereignty of God would become manifest. Qutb's separation of the Muslim community into believers and unbelievers was to be reinforced by Ayman al-Zawahiri, the intellectual leader of al-Qaeda, through the revival of the theory of "loyalty and separation."[15] According to this theory, true Muslims everywhere are to be supported, and there needs to be a radical separation from unbelievers at all levels. "Any person who deals with unbelievers even in private, betrays the unity and oneness of God and commits the greatest conceivable sin (*shirk*). The weapon for support and separation is the jihad. Qutb's theory of the sovereignty of God in the divided Muslim society is exacerbated through the commitment to universal assistance through violent jihad."[16] This ideology, which demands a violent struggle against the enemies of Islam, was further developed and promoted in an extreme form by the Egyptian Abd Al-Salam Faraj, who belonged to the circles that were behind the assassination of President Sadat.[17]

Schäfer comes to the following conclusion:

> Sunni Islam has spawned movements that according to my criteria are to be labelled fundamentalist. I would not apply this term to conservative Salafism. This is more of an enclave religion. It gives absolute status to its beliefs, but it does not seek to use them for the domination of society. The criteria apply to the Muslim Brotherhood and similar organizations. However, one needs to make distinctions according to the phases of activity and the

tendencies that are involved. When sections of the movement in the recent past have pursued the option of dialogue in political dialogue, they still have an interest in political domination, but they have put their absolutist religious claims to one side. They are developing into a kind of Islamic "Christian Democracy," which cannot be described as fundamentalist solely because of their basic religious orientation. Without question, the Salafist terrorist movements meet both criteria to a large extent.[18]

The other notable example of Islamic fundamentalism is the Iranian revolution in 1979.[19] One of the specific features of the Shiite tradition is the central role of the imam as a spiritual leader as a successor to the Prophet and the expectation that the Twelfth Imam, who has lived in occulation since 873, will return at the end of time as the Mahdi, a kind of messianic salvation figure. Shiite Islam also differs from Sunni Islam in the prominence it gives to ritual, especially the Ashura ritual, in which the faithful practise self-flagellation to identify themselves with the martyrdom of Imam Husayn at the Battle of Karbala. In the confrontation with the violent regime of the Shah and the search for a redefinition of Iranian identity in the conflict of modernization, Ayatollah Khomeini had recourse to these two elements. Based on the traditional authority of the *ulama* for Iranian believers, he developed the postulate of the "governorship of the Mahdi." This theory, which implies a claim not only to religious but also to political domination, picked up the "ancient doctrine of the future return of the hidden Twelfth Imam, the Mahdi, but blurs the boundaries between the future and the present. In portraying himself as the representative of the Mahdi on earth, he makes explicit the tradition's latent correlation between the Ayatollah and the omniscient Imam, thus creating the ideological conditions for a theocratic regime."[20] After Khomeini's death the fundamentalist strategy gradually evolved toward a regime with a republican constitution, in which the supreme spiritual leader remains, nevertheless, the ultimate authority. Under President Ahmadinejad, who left office in 2013, the fundamentalist option was given new emphasis, especially through the strategic use of apocalyptic elements in the Shiite tradition as a cosmic drama leading to the eschatological final battle against the anti-divine powers.

There are also fundamentalist movements in contemporary Judaism. Their development is related to the disputes over Jewish identity and particularly the identity of the State of Israel within the context of the Middle East conflict.[21] This is a case of a particular expression of a conflict about modernization being closely linked to the founding of the state. The Zionist project aimed at establishing a Western-style secular nation-state and, in the first three decades following the founding of Israel, political leadership was in the hands of socialist-oriented Zionists. Orthodox Judaism, which had been organized since 1912 in the Agudat Israel, saw this as betraying Jewish identity to Western modernity. From an Orthodox perspective, the return to Jerusalem and the promised land was linked to the coming of the Messiah. The decision to found the state was, from an Orthodox perspective, a "desecration" of the country and a denial of the absolute sovereignty of God over the fate of his people. The Orthodox factions thus withdrew into religious enclaves after the founding of the state and concentrated on building their own independent institutions.

However, there were also religious groups within the broader Zionist movement. In contrast to the secular majority, they advocated a religious identity for the new state, and organized themselves as the National Religious Party in 1956. They sought a political and social order for Israel based on the Torah and advocate strengthening the national religious institutions. In contrast to the orthodox Agudat, and its successor groups, they participate actively in the political process and were members of most coalition governments before 1977.

The underlying conflict that had existed since the founding of the State of Israel over whether the state should have a secular or a religious identity took on a new dimension following the Six-Day War of 1967, after which Israel occupied East Jerusalem, the

West Bank, the Golan Heights, and the Sinai Peninsula. In the eyes of religious Jews, and not only the Orthodox, most of the biblical land of "Eretz Israel" was now under Israeli control and the central religious hopes appeared to have been fulfilled. Then, after Israel only narrowly avoided defeat in the Yom Kippur War of 1973, the secular Zionist Labour Party lost the confidence of voters. With the election of Menachem Begin in 1977, the conservative nationalist party Likud participated in government for the first time, becoming a pole of attraction for the religious and nationalist factions.

This is the context in which the Gush Emunim movement was founded in 1974 by young supporters of the National Religious Party, for whom the party attitude on the issue of sovereignty over the occupied territories was too indecisive. They were supported in their religious and political objectives by Rabbi Meir Kahane and the Kach party he founded in 1974, as well as other representatives of militant Jewish nationalism.[22] Gush Emunim sees itself as a Zionist renewal movement, believing the establishment of the State of Israel to be an indirect promotion of the messianic redemption process. For Gush Emunim the whole of the "Eretz Israel" is holy land and thus, under no circumstances, should the occupied territories be given up. Gush Emunim attempted to present political leaders with a fait accompli through the construction of settlements—at first illegally—in the occupied territories, such as in Hebron. The movement acted without official recognition until 1984 and kept its distance from party politics. In 1983, members of Gush Emunim perpetrated an attack on an Islamic school in Hebron, and an alleged plan to blow up the Muslim shrines on the Dome of the Rock was thwarted before it could take place.

Although Gush Emunim with its fundamentalist ideology and in terms of its numbers represents only a minority in the religious political spectrum in Israel, the strategy of Jewish settlement in the occupied territories was extremely successful. The total number of settlers has grown to approximately 500,000 (including East Jerusalem), and no Israeli government can ignore the facts on the ground so created. With the founding of the Sephardic Orthodox party

Shas in 1984 the spectrum of religious parties that, unlike Gush Emunim, take part in the political process and serve in the changing coalition governments has shifted. The party's main aims are to enforce religious norms in social life and it follows a pragmatic, nonideological policy in foreign affairs. In 2009, all the religious parties together won 19 percent of the votes and 23 seats in the Israeli parliament, a loss of four compared to the previous election. Nearly half (11) went to Shas. The religious factor therefore plays an autonomous, albeit limited, role in the political process, and the fundamentalism of Gush Emunim remains, like the strategies of the New Christian Right in the United States, ultimately embedded in critical discourse in the public space.

As a final example, mention may be made of Hindu nationalism.[23] Those who follow a narrow definition of fundamentalism as being about making absolute religious convictions set down in scripture would not describe the Indian movements gathered under the banner of Hindutva as fundamentalist. And in fact, one could with equal justification speak of cultural chauvinism or of nationalism in a religious guise. In the Indian public debate one often speaks of "communalism," which refers to an ideology according to which the followers of a particular religion form a basic social, political, and economic unity, and which stresses the differences or even antagonism between these groups.

To examine whether the formal definition of fundamentalism proposed by Schäfer applies to these phenomena in India, the historical and religious context will be described in more detail. From the end of the 19th century the Indian independence movement included both radical nationalist movements, opposed not only to British rule but also directed against the Muslim minority, particularly in northern India, and a constitutionalist tendency that sought to construct a new national identity including all the minorities. The nationalist position made use of religious symbols from the very beginning. It not only tolerated the politicization of religious differences but used them for its own objectives. The foundation of modern India as a secular constitutional state giving the same rights to all religious, ethnic, and cultural minorities and tolerant of religious pluralism was intended to encourage an identity that transcends the differences by stressing social and economic development. This, of course, meant abstaining from giving a public role to religion, amounting to the *de facto* privatization of religion.

There was increasing resistance to this model of a secular state by the Hindu nationalist forces that had been brought together since the 1920s under the banner of Hindutva. One of the leaders of this movement, Vinayak Damodar Savarkar, had first presented his idea of a Hindu nation (Hindu Rashtra) in his 1923 publication, *Hindutva: Who Is a Hindu?* This identity was founded on the principles of the common sacred ground and a common ancestry and culture. This required, however, reconstructing an original Hindu nation, Bharata, to be defended against all forms of foreign domination through colonialism, and all religious traditions that did not develop out of Indian soil, especially Islam and Christianity. Of fundamental significance for the ideology of Hindutva promoted by Savarkar and his successors, especially Madhav Sadashiv Golwalkar, the leading ideologist of the militant organization Rashtriya Swayamsevak Sangh (RSS), founded in 1925, was the interpenetration of religion, culture, politics, and society.

In its public self-portrayal and official statements the Hindu nationalist ideology stresses that the movements of Hindutva, including the Bharatiya Janata Party (BJP) as its political representation, are directed to the defense of the Indian cultural heritage and not bound to a religious or political dogma. Of course, Indian cultural heritage is thoroughly influenced by religion, and the Western Enlightenment distinction between religion and culture is not applicable to India. The Indian religious tradition is nondogmatic and plural. It manifests itself primarily in a ritual religious practice that is grounded in the belief in the immutability of the all-determining *dharma*, that is, the sacred, cosmic order, and the resulting form of society, the caste system and cultic distinction between "pure" and "unpure." Where this religiously rooted conviction is made absolute, including the demand to withdraw civic rights from all those who do not profess the cultural and religious tradition of Hindutva, and where its quest for dominance and political hegemony is directed violently against Muslim and Christian minorities, the term *fundamentalism* in the sense of the formal definition applies.

The third criterion proposed by Schäfer, whereby the "context for such a strategy is the underlying politicization of all aspects of life through the process of modernization," particularly applies to the Indian context. In India, as in Israel and in other forms in Islamic states such as Egypt and Iran, the conflict linked to modernization has been politically instrumentalized through the founding of a (secular) nation-state. This requires renegotiating the relationship between religion and politics. Fundamentalism is the militant advocacy of the (re)creation of the original unity of religion, culture, and politics in the form of a religiously sanctioned sacred order, using the power of religious or pseudo-religious symbols for political mobilization in the public space. As in the other cases that have been examined, there is also a "moderate" wing of the movement in India, which campaigns within the framework of the constitution for a new understanding of Indian national identity and a social order that corresponds to this.

Fundamentalism and the Power of Religion in Society

The description and analysis in this chapter has located the rise of fundamentalist movements in the context of modernization conflicts, in which a traditional society becomes increasingly differentiated and as a result needs to redefine both its collective identity and the relationship between religion and politics. Chapter 1 investigated the secularization of state, culture, and society that is characteristic of European modernity. It became apparent that this form of secularization and the increasing removal of religion from the public space is the result of a particular historical dynamic in the relationship between state and church in Europe and needs to be distinguished from a general theory of modernization. The United States of America developed a different form of modernity, not resulting from the critical transformation of a traditional order, but as a religiously motivated act of revolution against a colonial regime, in other words the foundation of a new nation: "A modernity of quite a different kind to that in Europe developed in the United States: a revolutionary religious commonwealth of a reformed and free church tradition linked to an institutional separation of state and churches. Religious fundamentalism has an organic function in this specific form of modernity."[24]

Modernity developed under different historical and cultural conditions in the countries caught up in the modernization process over the last 50 years than it did in Europe and America. In most of these countries, religion and culture are still barely differentiated, at least in the lifeworld of the people. Seeing religion as a matter of private convictions would not do justice to a social reality that is still characterized by organizing principles and ideas rooted in religious traditions. This is reflected in the much-cited "resurgence of religion" and its demand for a public role and it comes into conflict with the Western model of a secular state inherited from the colonial era. Conflicts are inevitable where this is linked to a state-centred understanding of politics that aims at an all-encompassing claim to power and the concentration of power in the hands of the organs of the state. This is the context in which fundamentalist movements develop.

Common to all fundamentalist movements is that they perceive the secular understanding of the state and the public order as a threat to the religiously based collective identity and way of life for society that they demand. It is precisely because this identity and way of life is no longer taken for granted as a result of the process of modernization that it needs to be intentionally reconstructed. This is what distinguishes all forms of fundamentalism from mere traditionalism and makes fundamentalism a "modern" phenomenon.

Reconstruction takes shape around a central element of the tradition that is given an absolute and unchangeable value. This might be sacred scriptures or a divinely sanctioned legal order. The relationship to the land, a particular view of the world and its place in the end times, or the moral ordering of interpersonal relationships could become the object of such absolute convictions.

Fundamentalist movements strategically use the symbolic power of religions and consider all those who do not share their convictions as being not mere opponents but enemies that need to be defeated. They reject on principle the process of negotiation and the search for a new form of politics that recognizes the freedom and integrity of both dimensions and their significance for the life of society. They transform the conflict of interests in a plural society to conflicts over identity that can be resolved only through spiritually and religiously legitimized forms of struggle rather than through the tools of rational political debate.

At the beginning of this chapter we noted the difference between "private" and "public" religion that is characteristic for the United States of America, and for which Rainer Prätorius made the distinction between "Religion 1" and "Religion 2."[25] The privatization of religion in its denominational form is, in the United States, embedded in a universally religiously based understanding of collective identity founded on religious symbols. This equilibrium, which is characteristic for the cohesion of the American nation, could be maintained as long as the symbols borrowed from revivalist Protestantism were recognized as a shared civil religion by the various forms of Religion 1. This equilibrium has been disturbed, however, as a result of increasing conflict linked to modernization, on which the rise of fundamentalism is based. The combative and exclusive claim to a religious interpretation of the collective identity in terms of fundamentalist convictions—such as the proclamation of the United States as a "Christian nation" and tying the legal system to religiously based moral norms—challenges the fundamental principle of the separation of state and church, and of religion and politics. Thus even in the United States the relationship between religion and politics needs to be renegotiated, something that is happening primarily in the American courts.

American Protestant evangelical fundamentalism has changed its profile several times in the century since it first appeared, especially through the influence of charismatic and Pentecostal movements. What started as an internal conflict within Protestant denominations, particularly the Presbyterians, Baptists, and Methodists, has become a militant movement that seeks to lead public debate and to influence political and legal decisions, through coalitions with neoconservative tendencies, and alliances with conservative Roman Catholic and Orthodox Jewish groups. This is a show of power of public religion that in its most extreme forms aims to abolish the separation of church and state—or religion and politics—as set down in the U.S. Constitution, and to eliminate the traditional balance between "private" and "public" religion. The symbolic power of religion is thereby transformed into a strategic political force using all the means that the political system of the United States has at its disposal. American fundamentalism thus exploits the public space guaranteed by law and its openness to religious discourse. It attacks the modern assumption of the fundamental secularity of the public space, seeing this as a violation of the freedom of religion and the equal opportunities guaranteed by law. Observers differ, however, on whether the fundamentalist movements will succeed in achieving a fundamental change and transformation of the specifically American relationship between religion and politics.

Certainly the strategy of electoral mobilization means that fundamentalist movements must suspend their absolute convictions and positions in favour of a critical public discourse and thus are forced to accept compromise. This view is confirmed by the analysis of José Casanova, who sees in Protestant fundamentalism four possible postures: "a defensive reaction to protect the lifeworld of fundamentalists from outside encroachment, a proactive offensive to restore the American way of life, a counterrevolutionary theocratic impulse to impose biblical morality upon the nation, and a proactive involvement in the public affairs of the nation."[26] Only the fourth option, he believes, has any long-term prospects of success. He notes, though, that the logic of fundamentalism tends more to an "agonic" than a "discursive" model of public debate:

> Mobilizational and electoral success, however, require not only strategic adjustment to the rules and dynamics of the organizational society and electoral politics but also ideological compromises, which tend to undermine fundamentalist principles and identities. . . . The logic of open public discourse implies that modern societies, while protecting the free exercise of fundamentalism in the private sphere, procedurally cannot tolerate fundamentalism in the public sphere. Fundamentalism has to validate its claims through public argument.[27]

The analysis and assessment of the role of fundamentalism as a political religion in the American system of the political public sphere can help in assessing the issue of fundamentalism in other countries and in other world religions. In Islamic countries as well as in India the secular state and its legitimacy is at the centre of the conflict. This system rests on a far-reaching structural and legal separation of religion and politics with a tendency toward the privatization of religion. The system thus comes into conflict with the religious character of the lifeworld of the population, in which culture, religion, and politics are closely intertwined. The procedural legitimacy of the system that exists in the United States through elections and through the maintenance of a fundamental social consensus that creates identity in the wider public sphere cannot be taken for granted in these countries. Fundamentalism in its Islamic and Hindu forms fundamentally denies the legitimacy of the secular nation-state and strives for collective social and political identity to be refounded on a religious basis. The militant, potentially totalitarian logic of fundamentalism aims to eliminate the secular political system, if necessary by violent means. Conversely, it provokes authoritarian tendencies within the political system that further limit the already restricted room for democratic, public debate.

The example of India, which has developed a remarkably stable, democratic tradition that has been preserved despite numerous internal crises, demonstrates that the challenge of fundamentalism can be best met, however, in forcing such movements to engage in public political debate and to take part in the political process. Wherever fundamentalist movements, or their more moderate wings, have transformed themselves into political parties and have taken responsibility for specific political decisions, they have been forced to convert their uncompromising identity politics into a pragmatic balancing of conflicting interests. Such coercion is strengthened given the consequences of the global interdependence of all states and societies. Even the initially successful, fundamentalist strategy of the revolutionary transformation of Iran into a theocratic Islamic republic is reaching its limits both internally and in international relations. Differentiated and pluralistic societies that rely on international cooperation and economic exchange cannot in the long run remain subject to an exclusive normative religious order. On the other hand, the experience of these countries shows that the secular state model fails to provide a stable base for the formation of a collective identity. The symbolic power of religions, which points to a source of legitimacy that transcends all powers and ideologies, proves to be a factor in the formation of individual and collective identity that politics must not neglect.

Fundamentalism in its various forms is a manifestation, in sometimes extreme forms, of the public power of religion in society and thereby challenges the secular identity of Western modernity. The models developed in Western countries to distinguish between and to relate religion and politics cannot be applied here. At best, criteria may be formulated that allow a sustainable relationship between religion and politics. This applies particularly to the question of the role of religion in the search for a new world order, to which the final chapter will turn.

5. Religion, Power, and Politics

Legitimacy Problems in the World of States

Do religions have a specific contribution to make in the quest for a new world order? Or do religions need to be kept as far as possible from efforts to reshape international relations because of their role in unleashing or at least exacerbating many of today's global conflicts? This was the question underlying this attempt to subject the relationship between religion and politics to a more thorough analysis. What are the results of this analysis and what conclusions may be drawn?

We seem to be dealing with a fundamental change in the way in which politics is understood and practiced, in both the national and the international context, and which has its origins in the changing role of the state as the basic model for the coexistence of society. The prevailing understanding of politics in European modernity is based on the state as the apparatus of governance, particularly associated with the acquisition and exercise of power (Machiavelli, Hobbes). This has led to a "secularization" of politics compared to the traditional understanding of politics and ethics (or religion) in antiquity (especially in Aristotle), and to which the secular conception of the state and its sovereignty corresponds.

The classical approach, based on a system of sovereign nation-states, is now open to question and not only because of how it understands politics. The study of developments in the Islamic world and of fundamentalist movements in all religions demonstrates that it is the *secular* understanding of the state and of politics that is at the centre of many of the conflicts and disputes over religion and politics. According to the analysis of Mark Juergensmeyer there are two competing models of social order at play, one based on the theory and practice of the secular nation-state, the other based on the tradition of a cultural and religious foundation for collective, political, and social identity. Both claim to offer an all-encompassing basis for legitimate authority in politics and society. This makes clear that a central issue in the tension between politics and religion is the question of the social order and its legitimacy.

A central task of the state, in the classic paradigm of the sovereign nation-state, is seen as the maintenance of law and order. Sovereignty in external relations means the right to enforce national interests, if necessary by using military force, and to ward off any intervention and interference in internal affairs. It is against this background that Max Weber formulates his understanding of politics, mentioned in chapter 1, seen as the leadership of a state as a "human community that (successfully) claims the *monopoly of the legitimate use of physical force* within a given territory."[1]

The monopoly of force and the power and ability to decide on and to enforce law are still key features of state order. In political theory, the basis of legitimacy for this claim to effective sovereignty is based on a "social contract" through which the people as the "sovereign" provide the state order with the necessary authority. In constitutional democracies, the legitimacy of the political order is based on the constitution as an expression of this fundamental social consensus, and regularly reaffirmed through the process of electing representative decision-making bodies. In the majority of the new nation-states of the southern hemisphere, this secular understanding of legitimate state order, on which all proposals for a new world order are based, encounters traditions that tie the legitimacy of the social and political order to conformity with the religious and moral values engrained in the culture.

This results in a crucial dilemma for efforts to create a new world order. Most of the new nation-states in the South lack a developed democratic public culture providing a social consensus on which to base the legitimate exercise of political authority, and thus both internal and external sovereignty. On top of this, the nation-state and its organs often appear to be structures for the pure exercise of domination by an elite that wishes to maintain or increase its power. Several examples in this study have demonstrated that religions can become the central source for an autonomous culture of civil society. However, when it comes to the efforts so far to create a new world order, there is an even greater lack of a public culture and of a "social contract." The main actors remain the nation-states, with questionable legitimacy at the very least. Despite the steps taken to create an international legal order and to appeal to a basic set of human rights that precede or transcend the state, efforts so far remain trapped in the "world of states." The transition to a "world of societies," where the actors are the peoples and the nations, remains a utopia. All efforts so far to create a new world order have suffered not only from a lack of coherence, but above all from a democratic deficit, and linked to this, a fundamental deficit of legitimacy.

We thus need to return to the normative and ethical issues with which the introduction concludes. The approaches it discusses about a new concept of international politics that attempts to link political realism directed to the "world of states" with fundamental moral and ethical principles means developing a political ethics of responsibility. Politics so conceived as being directed toward the wider perspective of the political public sphere needs to free itself from traditional ideas of power and domination and to be open to public discourse and decision making through negotiation. This is particularly the case when it comes to seeking a consensus on the moral and ethical foundations that can offer legitimacy to a new world order beyond legal, formal, and procedural criteria. The approach adopted by secular efforts for a new world order needs to face the critique and enter into debate with the perspectives seeking a viable order of coexistence of people and nations that are alive in humanity's cultural and religious traditions.

Order, Power, and Violence

The power to sanction and enforce is constitutive for state order. According to Max Weber's definition, "the monopoly of legitimate physical force" is part of what state order means. Erhard Eppler demonstrates his basic agreement with this definition in noting that "when a state has lost its monopoly of force ... it has ceased to exist as a state."[2] The monopoly of force in the hands of a state, or of its officials, is thus the most cogent definition of state power and domination. Max Weber has in mind his often-cited definition of power and domination. Power, according to his basic sociological terminology, "is the probability that one actor within a social relationship will be in a position to carry out his own will despite resistance, regardless of the basis on which this probability rests." Domination, on the other hand, "is the probability that a command with a given specific content will be obeyed by a given group of persons." And he adds, by way of explanation: "The concept of power is sociologically amorphous. All conceivable qualities of a person and all conceivable combinations of circumstances may put him in a position to impose his will in a given situation. The sociological concept of domination must hence be more precise and can only mean the probability that a *command* will be obeyed."[3]

As far as the nation-state is concerned, power, according to Weber, is *legitimate domination*, as far as it rests "on a belief in the legality of enacted rules and the right of those elevated to authority under such rules to issue commands."[4] The expectation that an order will produce obedience, characteristic for a relation of domination, refers in the case of a state to the binding nature of the legal order. Eppler explains this through reference to Paul Tillich, who defined the state as a "community tempered by justice."[5] According to Tillich,

> The state is the bearer of justice, and where justice is upheld, there is the state.... But at the same time, the state requires a community that has the power of justice, power over itself which it

reveals in positing its justice. Where there is no intrinsic power (*Selbstmächtigkeit*) there is no state. Where there is no power to posit and to enforce justice there is no state. In the development of the state, the power of a community obtains form, and thereby existence. The state is the power of a community that realizes itself in the positing of justice.[6]

We shall return in the next section to the specific issue of the relationship between power, law, and morality. Here it is primarily a matter of demonstrating that the dominant understanding of political and social order, and thus of a viable "world order," continues to be influenced by the categories and criteria of state order. The rule of law requires the existence of a power that can define and enforce law. Up until now, international law has been law based on treaties between states; the effective power of enforcement remains with the states. Even the judgments of the International Court of Justice gain validity only when they are accepted by the states concerned. The existing international order is thus, in principle, "anarchistic": there is no structure of governance with the legitimate expectation that its orders will be met by obedience.

For this study, however, it is significant that the sentences quoted above from Tillich point to a shift in emphasis when compared to Weber's classical definition. Weber developed his definition from the perspective of a governing elite. In such a perspective, society, that is, human beings as citizens, appear only as the subjects of domination, understood as orders, obedience, and "physical force." Ultimately, this is also the case for Weber's definition of power as the ability to carry out one's own will despite resistance, and thus as "power over" others, who have only to comply and to conform. According to Weber, the willingness and ability to use force is a constitutive element of the state. In his lecture on politics as a vocation, he states: "Like the political institutions historically preceding it, the state is a relation of men dominating men, a relation supported by means of legitimate (i.e. considered to be legitimate) violence."[7] This concept of absolute power has accompanied the rise of the European nation-state since the time of Thomas Hobbes and has influenced the classical understanding of sovereignty.

In contrast, Tillich speaks of the "power of a community" expressing its intrinsic power in the positing of justice. The state is not opposed to society as an apparatus of domination. Instead, it is the power of community that finds its expression in the state. Tillich thus picks up a tradition of political theory and understanding of the power that goes back to the Greek *polis* and that came into play again during the American Revolution.

In her book *On Violence* Hannah Arendt impressively develops this second understanding of power.[8] She points to "the concept of power and law whose essence did not rely on the command-obedience relationship and which did not identify power and rule or law and command." For the American revolutionaries when they created their republic, it was a question of constituting "a form of government . . . where the rule of law, resting on the power of the people, would put an end to the rule of man over man."[9] She continues: "It is the people's support that lends power to the institutions of a country, and this support is but the continuation of the consent that brought the laws into existence to begin with. . . . All political institutions are manifestations and materializations of power: they petrify and decay as soon as the living power of the people ceases to uphold them."[10]

Arendt insists on the need to distinguish clearly between power, strength, force, authority, and violence. She defines power as corresponding "to the human ability not just to act but to act in concert. Power is never the property of an individual; it belongs to the group and remains in existence only so long as the group keeps together. When we say of somebody that he is 'in power' we actually refer to his being empowered by a certain number of people to act in their name. The moment the group, from which the power originated to begin with . . . disappears, 'his power' also vanishes."[11] In her earlier book *The Human Condition*, Arendt points out that the word *power* itself, like its Greek equivalent *dynamis*, the Latin *potentia*, and its modern derivatives, indicates possibility, and thus its "potential" character.[12]

Power is therefore, in contrast to strength, not an individual characteristic or quality: it is bound to the social relationship and develops in communication and cooperation. According to Arendt, it is all the more important to make a clear distinction between power and violence:

> Power is indeed of the essence of all government, but violence is not. Violence is by nature instrumental; like all means, it always stands in need of guidance and justification through the end it pursues. . . . Power needs no justification, being inherent in the very existence of political communities: what it does need is legitimacy. Power springs up whenever people get together and act in concert, but it derives its legitimacy from the initial getting together rather than from any action that might follow.[13]

Summing up her differentiated analysis, Arendt states that "politically speaking, it is insufficient to say that power and violence are not the same. Power and violence are opposites: where the one rules absolutely, the other is absent. Violence appears where power is in jeopardy, but left to its own course it ends in power's disappearance. . . . Violence can destroy power: it is utterly incapable of creating it."[14] Even more pointedly, she notes that there is no quantitative or qualitative transition from power to violence. Power cannot be derived from violence, just as violence cannot be derived from power; power is not the soft form of violence, nor violence the most extreme manifestation of power.[15]

Arendt's approach, which has been cited here extensively because of its incisiveness and cogency, has exerted a lasting influence on later discussions about the issues of social norms, power, and violence, going beyond the perspectives developed by Weber.[16] In his definition of power and the exercise of power, Weber concentrates on the constitutive elements of all political order. The starting point for Arendt, on the other hand, is power as a fundamental dimension of all interaction in social groups. This does not exclude political and state power, but her interpretation of authority as the "empowerment" of a leader by the group reflects an understanding of politics and the state that is not built on command and obedience, and thus not on power as dominion "over" others, but on the ability to cooperate and communicate "with" others to build and to promote an order based on rules and the rule of law.

The critical distinction between the two concepts is their attitude to violence and the associated question of the legitimacy of power and social or political order. Weber focuses, as previously demonstrated, on the legality of systems based on positive law, which "is externally guaranteed by the probability that physical or psychological coercion will be applied by a *staff* of people to bring about compliance or avenge violation."[17] Even Arendt links the legitimacy of power and order to the rule of law, which for her is rooted in the collective will and the basic consensus of the community or the nation. Power that makes use of the means of violence undermines its fundamental basis.

In the further discussion, it became clear that Weber and Arendt represent two poles in the understanding of power and order. Both tend to reduce their theories to one central aspect and neither of the two definitions can claim to capture all facets of the complex reality of power. In addition to state and social power, a contemporary analysis needs to take account of the new forms of economic, technological, scientific, military, media, as well as cultural and symbolic power. Alongside the understanding of power as domination "over" others (Weber) and power as a common will to act "with" others (Arendt), we need to include the definitions of power as the ability "to" undertake effective action or for the cooperative orientation and implementation of decisions.[18] Power may also be defined as the ability to make use of certain assets or resources, such as capital, property, knowledge, status, communication, but also instruments of violence to achieve results. This corresponds to the suggestion from Carl Friedrich von Weizsäcker that power should be defined "as the accumulation of assets for purposes that have been left open."[19]

More helpful for our discussion is Jürgen Habermas's suggestion that we distinguish between political and social power, and then, as far as political power is concerned, to differentiate between communicative and administrative power. Political power is constituted and develops in the forms of law, while social power is the ability to enforce one's own interests effectively.[20] Habermas refers explicitly to Arendt's considerations discussed above, when he states:

> In contrast to Weber, who sees the fundamental phenomenon of power as the probability that in a social relationship one can assert one's own will against opposition, Arendt views power as the potential of a *common will* formed in noncoercive communication.... Arendt conceives political power neither as a potential for asserting one's own interests or for realizing collective goals, nor as the administrative power to implement collectively binding decisions, but rather as an *authorizing* force expressed in "jurisgenesis"—the creation of legitimate law—and in the founding of institutions.[21]

Using the concept of "communicative power," Habermas picks up Arendt's theories, but also shows that the real issues concerning the exercise, distribution, and competition over power have not been sufficiently clarified. Therefore, as far as political power is concerned, one needs to differentiate between communicative power and administrative power:

> The concept of communicative power requires a differentiation in the concept of political power. Politics cannot coincide as a whole with the practice of those who talk to one another in order to act in a politically autonomous manner. The exercise of political autonomy implies the discursive formation of a common will, not the implementation of the laws issuing therefrom. The concept of the political in its full sense *also* includes the use of administrative power within the political system, as well as the competition for access to that system.... This leads me to propose that we view law as the medium through which communicative power is translated into administrative power.... We can then interpret

the idea of the constitutional state in general as the requirement that the administrative system, which is steered through the power code, be tied to the lawmaking communicative power and kept free of illegitimate interventions of social power (i.e., of the factual strength of privileged interests to assert themselves).[22]

Taking account of these considerations of Habermas about the differentiated analysis of politics and of political power, we can return to the issue of the foundation of the legitimacy of social and political order. Here we have to deal with the relationship between power, law, and morality.

POWER, LAW, AND MORALITY

In their studies, Weber and Habermas show how legal and moral rules gradually became distinct entities in the process of moving from prestate tribal societies to the founding of early states.[23] Both sets of rules developed from the behavioural standards of a community transmitted through the generations and usually rooted in religion. Law and morality have the same origin and, just as politics and religion, remained related to each other throughout long historical periods. Morality, on the one hand, represents the fundamental principles and inner connection of the rules and modes of behaviour that express the collective self-understanding of a community. Law, on the other hand, seeks institutionally safeguarded structures of enforceable rules and obligations that allow orderly cooperation and ensure that conflicts of interest and power are able to be resolved, thereby establishing a social order.[24] Law and morality are thus complementary. In both cases the aim is to maintain a viable community order that promotes coexistence. Both base their legitimacy on an all-encompassing, sacred or religiously founded order of the lifeworld. The review in chapter 3 on the process of creating an institutional framework in the Muslim community and the formation of Islamic law is a good example of the way in which law and morality are both related to, and differentiated from, each other. Frank Crüsemann has tracked the same process in examining the sociohistorical development of law and state order in ancient Israel. As far as the ways in which political power is expressed, the function of law is to bind the exercise of power to the fundamental principles of morality, and, in particular, to the principle of justice. The law therefore mediates between politics and morality.

When the notions of the relationship between power, law, and morality that have been sketched out here, at least in rudimentary form, are applied to the issue of the basis of the legitimacy of a new world order, then we need to concentrate on the recognition of human rights and compliance with the "rule of law." The concept of "rule of law" was already expressed in the ideal of a political order discussed in Greek antiquity in which, as Arendt said in reference to the American Revolution, "the rule of law, resting on the power of the people, would put an end to the rule of man over man."[25]

The "rule of law" is now increasingly seen as a crucial element for good governance at national and international level. According to the definition of the International Commission of Jurists at its Congress in New Delhi in 1959 the "rule of law" is based on the "principles, institutions and procedures, not always identical but broadly similar, which the experience and traditions of lawyers in different countries of the world, often having themselves varying political structures and economic backgrounds, have shown to be important to protect the individual from arbitrary government and to enable him to enjoy the dignity of man."[26]

Through its reference to human dignity, this definition of the concept of the "rule of law" includes an implicit reference to human rights. In fact, the respect for and effective implementation of human rights is a key criterion for the "rule of law." The preamble to the Universal Declaration of Human Rights of 1948 underlines that "if man is not to be compelled to have recourse, as a last resort, to rebellion against tyranny and oppression, . . . human rights should be protected by the rule of law" and that "recognition of the inherent dignity and of the equal and inalienable rights of all members of the human family is the foundation of freedom, justice and peace in the world."[27] A world order that is sustainable in the sense of the "rule of law" must therefore be built on the fundamental principles of human rights and respect for human dignity. All binding international legal instruments and norms need to be based on these principles.

The two International Covenants on Civil and Political and Economic, Social and Cultural Rights of 1966 and 1976 translated the objectives of the Universal Declaration of Human Rights into binding international law. The additional optional protocols and additional Conventions and the Statute of the International Court of 1998 have given weight to the efforts to bind the exercise of state power to the norms that precede or transcend the state. But the guardians of world order, that is, the organs of the United Nations, still lack the "administrative power" for the global enforcement of human rights and respect for human dignity and to impose sanctions where these principles are violated. This also applies to the newly formed Human Rights Council and the instruments at its disposal. There remains a strong temptation to use human rights as a political or ideological instrument in the struggle to enforce geopolitical power interests.

In their book *Where Needs Meet Rights*, the Dutch jurists Baas de Gaay Fortman and Berma Klein Goldewijk have subjected the traditional human-rights discourse to critical analysis with the aim of working out the constructive potential of the concept of human rights in the quest for a new world order.[28] They focus primarily on a new interpretation of economic, social, and cultural rights. Their investigation is guided by the conviction that the official human-rights discourse is too state-centred, focussing primarily on civil and political rights and their legal enforceability within the state order.

They propose an alternative approach that does not place rights but basic human needs at the fore: the satisfaction of human needs has to be understood as a comprehensive goal of social action as an overriding interest. Human needs are, so to speak, the "other side" of human dignity, that is, humanity and decent life are manifested not least in requiring and being dependent upon recognition in the human community. Where basic human needs are not met, there is a violation and degradation of human dignity. The term *human rights* therefore denotes both entitlements to basic freedoms and the legitimate expectation that needs will be satisfied. Thus understood, human dignity must be regarded as being at the centre of a human-rights discourse that emanates from the needs for decent life and not only from the requirements of the rule of law.[29]

If the inner core of the basis of legitimacy for a new world order is that of human rights at the centre of the "rule of law" and respect for human dignity, then it becomes clear why the relationship between religion and politics takes on a particular intensity. Human rights as set out in the human-rights declarations and conventions of the United Nations and other intergovernmental organizations clearly express a secular understanding of politics and government. The state-centred character of the official discourse on human rights is underlined by the way in which they are directed mainly toward the rights of the individual person and the fact that their validity is subject to the consent of the states that have agreed to them. This discourse considers human rights from the perspective of states and their political responsibilities; the requirements for a decent life take second place.

The internal logic of such an understanding of human rights means that the only place for religious traditions is in terms of religious freedom, which in many cases is also reduced to the freedom of belief and conscience. The problematic development of the discussions on religious freedom was discussed at the end of chapter 2. For too long it has focused too one-sidedly on dealing with the issues and potential problems that arise in the relationship between organized religion and the state order. The strict separation of church and state, or politics and religion, is often taken for granted as a prerequisite for granting full religious freedom. Even when this does not include a tendency toward or the legal implications of a privatization of religion, it remains an open question as to whether religions, as advocates of the moral traditions of the peoples and nations, could and should contribute to providing a foundation for the legitimacy of the state order and, if so, what form this should take.

Human rights, and thus the freedom of religion that they guarantee, are, like all rights, situated on the boundary between politics and morality. As an expression of suprapositive law as a key reference point for the "rule of law," they are the foundation of the legal order, and thus are legally exercised state power. At the same time, they point to a broader moral order and thus express the awareness of justice and thereby a task of shaping political behaviour (*ein Gestaltungsauftrag*) against which all exercise of power needs to be critically measured. This second dimension of human rights comes into play when human dignity, and particularly legally formulated demands for freedom, equality, and participation, is recognized as the morally relevant core of human rights. The concept of "human dignity" has its roots in ancient philosophy as well as in the biblical statement that all human beings are created in the image of God. These two traditions were interwoven with each other at the time of the Enlightenment, which saw human dignity as being founded on the capacity for reason. Human dignity was the foundation of human autonomy and marked the difference between human beings and nature. On the other hand, human dignity was the criterion for the natural equality of all human beings. The understanding of human dignity described above, however, stresses the relational nature of human dignity that points to a relationship of recognition that supports life as a whole. Thus Wolfgang Huber states: "Human dignity takes shape in coexistence. Human rights in the service of human dignity can also be measured by how far they promote coexistence. In this respect human rights are not only defensive rights of the individual against the state but also, simultaneously, tasks in shaping political behaviour."[30]

When it comes to shaping decent life and coexistence in the community, then cultural and moral, as well as religious, traditions come into play. The contemporary concept of human rights based on respect for inalienable human dignity is repeatedly subjected to the critique that it claims universal validity for a specific cultural and religious understanding of the order of human life and society. This critique was raised by Asian representatives at the international Conference on Human Rights of the United Nations in Vienna (1993), who referred to the historical, cultural, and religious specificities of their region. They advocated the primacy of the rights of the community and social harmony over individual rights. On the other hand, representatives of Islamic states referred to the "The Cairo Declaration on Human Rights in Islam" of 1990, discussed in chapter 3, which defines *sharia* as the sole basis for human rights.[31] European intellectuals with a postmodernist orientation have also argued repeatedly that the fact that the modern concept of human rights has its roots in the European-American tradition stands in the way of its universal validity. Despite such objections, the final document of the Vienna conference restates the universality and indivisibility of human rights.

After analyzing various foundations for human rights and the tendency to relativize their validity, Huber comes to the conclusion: "Human rights need to be formulated in a way that they are open to a plurality of possible foundations (*begründungsoffen*). They lend themselves to an open, relative universality. The dialogue between the various Christian confessions, between the various world religions, and between religious and secular standpoints about the foundation and understanding of human rights is itself an important contribution to the protection and realization of human rights."[32] The results of recent interreligious dialogue, especially that between representatives of Christian churches and of the Muslim community, presented at the conclusion of chapter 3, show that it is possible to reach an understanding on human rights and human dignity despite differences of religious traditions. This could and should be an important contribution of religions to the construction of a new world order. We will return to this in the concluding section.

POLITICAL AND RELIGIOUS ACTION IN THE PUBLIC SPACE

At the beginning of this chapter, the broader understanding of politics was summarized by saying that "politics" encompasses all purposeful action in the public space. We now need to use this as a starting point to develop criteria to distinguish between political and religious action.[33]

This understanding of politics was based on the insight that the field of politics can no longer be restricted solely to the state and state functions. The political society and the civil society exist alongside the institutional political system of the state. Together they constitute the "public space." The survey of the different forms of "public religion" has shown that religious communities may enter the field of politics at all three levels: (1) as organizations analogous to the state and in their legal form directly related to the state; (2) as organizations such as political parties that seek to influence political decision-making processes; or (3) as groups within civil society participating in influencing public opinion and decision making and thereby influencing the objectives of political action.

Thus understood, the public space is the space in which communicative power, as understood by Arendt and Habermas, is formed and organized. It is the space of influencing public opinion and decision making in the context of civil society, but also the space in which specific political interests are expressed through the groupings of the political society. The state is different from the other actors in the public space due to the inherent administrative power that it is granted by virtue of the laws created as a result of communicative power. Within this sphere of the law, the state or its organs act in the interest of the common good as a "coercive organization" (Dieter Conrad). State action differs from other forms of purposeful action in the public sphere through its binding nature, that is, the authority to enforce "compulsory reinforced norms" and regulations. The state can enforce compliance with its instructions and decisions in the interest of public order even against resistance, sometimes using the resources of physical coercion or violence. Through its monopoly of force or violence, state political action is fundamentally different from all other forms of purposeful political action in the public space. This is the abiding, albeit limited law of the Weberian definition of the state. The previous considerations on power, law, and morality, have shown that the legitimacy of state political action, however, is not guaranteed simply by its legality. It is dependent upon, and must be continually reestablished through, the processes of forming communicative power. This is reflected in the requirement that the organs of state, in their exercise of administrative power, have an obligation to be accountable to the public, and to those affected by their actions.

Such a portrayal of political action on the part of state institutions through identifying the differences and interaction between communicative and administrative power, allows the possibility of describing the wider public space as the field of communicative political action.[34] Here it is not primarily about the binding enforcement of normative rules and decisions, but about influencing public opinion and decision making, as well as the controversial debate about the principles and orientation of community order. This is where the debate about issues of collective identity should take place, as about the related issue of the ethical and moral legitimacy of the social order. The entry of religion into the public space happens according to the rules of communicative action, where religions act as guardians of the communicative power of the symbols and rituals that make possible meaning and ways to deal with contingency by pointing to the transcendent source of power and legitimacy of all human order. All religions preserve an awareness of the universal principles of justice, peace, solidarity, and reciprocity as the basis of human society. The Golden Rule that exists in all religions can serve a criterion to distinguish religious action from forms of political action in the public sphere.

This applies particularly to distinguishing religious action from the political action of the state and its exercise of binding administrative power that is characterized by the monopoly of force and violence. Both state institutions and religions act in the public space, since both aim at the common good, and both are concerned with preserving a viable order for the human community. They differ in terms of their mode of action. "Insofar as politics, despite all the accretions and increasing complexity of what it deals with and its modes of control, remains ultimately characterized by state domination and the possibility of external coercion up to and including violence, the crucial political question to religion is not its public character, its relation to the world, or its private inwardness, but 'Where do you stand on violence?'"[35] This means, therefore, that religious action, for the sake of its integrity, needs to disengage itself from all systems of political coercion, "from state violence just as from resistance or counter-violence."[36] This is the abiding reason for demanding the separation of religion and politics in the sense of the political functions of the state. On the other hand, the broader understanding of politics as the various forms of communicative action in the public space demands the active participation of religions in the processes of developing communicative power as a critical counterweight to the administrative power of the organs of the state. As the guardians of symbolic power, and as advocates of the transcendent origin of the legitimacy of human order and integrity that transcends all sectional interests, they underline the political quality of the public space.

The particular field of action of public religion is the complementary relationship between law and morality that has already been discussed. The communicative power of a community is articulated in the process of law making. But all law making points to the principles that precede law (*vorrechtliche Prinzipien*) in which moral awareness is expressed through a just order. The positivist separation of law and morality and the foundation of the legitimacy of a legal order solely on the basis of the principles of the legality of "due process" and the rationality of law is a consequence of the secularist understanding of the state and politics. The reference to the "rule of law" as a feature of the primacy of the legal order in a community binds the question of legitimacy to respect for human dignity and the realization of human rights. Human rights are the form in which awareness of the universal moral order is expressed, as reflected in the diverse traditions of religions within a secular constitution of the community.

For the sake of the legitimacy of the legal order and its critical and constructive role toward politics, the constitutive connection between law and morality needs to be maintained. At the same time the plural nature of the public space requires a critical distinction between law and (religiously based) morality. Not everything that is morally required within a religious tradition can and should be translated into legally binding rules valid for all members of the community. Even the suprapositive principles of law making and legal determination need to be formulated in a way that they are open to "a plurality of possible foundations." This demand needs to be maintained vis-à-vis positions, for example, that bind the application of human rights to specifically religious foundations, as well as to attempts to limit the discourse exclusively to the arguments of secular reason as a matter of principle. As mentioned in chapter 1, Habermas argues for the recognition in public discourse of the untapped "cognitive and moral heritage of religions."[37] For this to be realized, however, there is a need for the freedom of religion and the recognition of the place of religion in the public space, and the absence of legal or political privileges for one religious community over against another. On the other hand, it means that religions, their followers, and their leaders can make a credible and effective contribution to the discourse on the legitimacy of the social order at the national and international level only if they renounce claims to absolute and universal authority, and engage in dialogue with each other and with the secular public sphere.

Religions as Advocates for a Culture of Dialogue and Peace

Efforts to build a new world order have until now focused mainly on the creation of legal, political, and administrative structures. Their legitimacy continues to be based primarily, as we have shown, on the desire of states to cooperate. In reality, they are not supported by the firm determination of the "peoples of the United Nations," of which the Preamble to the Charter of the United Nations speaks. They lack democratic legitimacy through a decision of the "people and nations," in which the "public interest" of the human community is expressed. There is not as yet any equivalent to a "social contract" at the global level.

Following the discussion in the previous sections, we can now say that the administrative political power necessary to establish and to enforce a new world order is weak because it is not supported and legitimized by communicative power, that is to say, by influencing public opinion and the decision making of the "peoples and nations." Thus proposals for a new world order, including the constitutive human-rights conventions, appear to be more an expression of the paramount interests of those sections of the international community that possess political, economic, and military power than the result of the development of the common will of the people and nations, and as an expression of a global "public interest." The transition from the "world of states" to a "world society" is not yet complete. To many people it appears not as a transition toward a new form of order in the coexistence of people and nations, but as a potential threat to the very foundations of social order.

All forms of social order are viable and sustainable only to the extent that they are embedded and supported by a culture that expresses the self-understanding and collective identity of the society in question. We thus need to transcend the previous analytical framework of "legality" and "legitimacy." "Culture" here refers to the relationship between attitudes, symbols, artistic expressions, tools, rules of conduct, moral values, and institutions through which a given community structures its social relations, its relationship to nature, to other communities, and to the world in general. In such a perspective, religious beliefs, symbols, and rituals are an integral part of the culture of a community. Cultures are not self-contained, timeless structures; they develop and change through processes of learning and socialization from one generation to the next, and they are influenced by other cultures. Thus new cultural patterns develop that in the long term contribute to changing and reorientating cultural identities. At the same time, the previous influences on identity remain part of the collective long-term memory.

Through the process of modernization and globalization, societies in all parts of the world are facing profound and conflict-laden cultural change. The secular culture of Western modernity, whose assumptions and values are also shaping moves toward a new world order, is coming into conflict with traditional cultures. Chapters 3 and 4 examined some examples of these conflicts. In many societies, enforced adaptation of the social order to increasing economic and political interdependence is not yet supported by a corresponding change in cultural awareness. There is no consensus about the guiding values and goals on which society should be based. Resistance against what is perceived as an alien order may lead to secessionist movements of smaller or larger groups fighting for the preservation of their ethnic and religious culture. It can also manifest itself as a political ideological movement, seeking radical and, under some circumstances, revolutionary changes in society while using religiously supported patterns of collective identity. If structures of political and social order possess only weak legitimacy, then those in power may be tempted to portray conflicts over access to power and resources as disputes about what constitutes cultural and religious identity.

It is in such situations of conflict-laden cultural change that the presence of religion in the public sphere and thus the relationship between religion and politics gives cause for critical reflection. In most of the societies so affected it is religious traditions that continue to provide the core of traditional culture and therefore the ultimate legitimacy for the social order. Thus religious symbols, rituals, and moral stipulations become the focal points for the defense or revival of cultural identity. In the absence of a legally protected public space and corresponding structures for civil society, the guardians of religious traditions are drawn into political controversies that revolve around demands for power and authority by a particular cultural and sectional interest. Religious traditions become exclusive markers of identity whose defense against alien influence is seen as a "sacred" duty. The conflicts that result are often seen by the wider public as being religious conflicts. Religions, which are often linked to particular cultures, or ethnic and national identities, appear to be the main reason why social peace is endangered. Of course, it can be correctly pointed out that in these conflicts it is a question of who has the power to shape the social order and not about the exclusive validity of religious traditions. Nevertheless, there are many examples where religious traditions and their leaders have allowed themselves to be instrumentalized, particularly in mobilizing their members to take one side in the conflict. Most strategies for the peaceful resolution of conflict will have little effect where a social and political dispute that could, in principle, be resolved through compromise becomes a radically antagonistic struggle about ultimate values and religious convictions. Religions represent a power potential in society and thus are part of the ambivalence of power as domination of human beings by other human beings.

All this applies not least to the conflict-laden encounter of different cultures at the global level. The secular culture of Western modernity that underlies the existing conceptions of a new world order is increasingly provoking resistance from traditional cultures. Certainly, new hybrid cultural forms that express an increasing cosmopolitan awareness are also developing in this environment. Such cultural forms remain detached and minimalist: they do not reach the depths of the "thick" cultural awareness that takes shape in traditional morality and in religious symbols and rites.[38] Cultural transformation and adaptation as a result of the processes of modernization do not erase the collective memory in which the remembrance of the deeper layers of identity have been preserved. A new world order must therefore take the continued existence of such patterns of identity into account and should not be made dependent upon the universal acceptance of a "cosmopolitan" culture. Rather, it needs to develop rules for a "dialogue of cultures" that are able to open a communicative "public space" and to protect it against sectional claims to religious and cultural hegemony, so that the "thick" cultural traditions are able to encounter and respect each other. Research by Hans Küng has shown that the "Golden Rule" is deeply rooted in the various religious and cultural traditions of humanity. The "Declaration Toward a Global Ethic"[39] builds on this in proclaiming the Golden Rule as the basic standard for human coexistence and as the basis for commitment to a "culture" of nonviolence, solidarity, tolerance, and equality. Here, of course, "culture" is not be understood as the "thick" cultural awareness of a particular community but, rather, as a reference to a framework of regulatory principles protecting a communicative public space.[40] So understood, human rights also offer basic regulatory principles for the global public space. In the dialogue of cultures and religions, communication and the discourse about motivations and relationships with existing cultural and religious traditions need to be promoted and deepened.

Thus we have reached the point at which we need to draw conclusions from the preceding analysis on power, law, and morality and the criteria for distinguishing between political and religious action. Where the symbolically based power of religions is transformed into antagonistic political power, it loses its authority rooted in transcendence and becomes the ideological legitimization of sectional interests. It thus becomes subordinate to the friend-enemy opposition and violates the basic precept of the Golden Rule. All religions face the temptation of using their symbolic power as an instrument to exercise political domination up to and including legitimizing the use of violence. There are clear historical and contemporary examples of this. They not only endanger the viability of political order, but they undermine their own integrity. We cannot do without the 17th-century principle of distinguishing between religion and politics that developed as a reaction to this danger, not only to protect the peace of society, but also for the freedom and integrity of the religions themselves and their authority for the coexistence of human society. This is also true for efforts to build a new world order.

On the other hand, the study has led to the conclusion that the secularist interpretation of the separation of religion and politics is based on assumptions which cannot be applied to other historical and cultural contexts nor on the global level. Here, the relationship between religion and politics must be renegotiated for the sake of the legitimacy of the social order. This conflict-laden process is currently underway and it should not be expected that a normative model will prevail. In any event, those who hold political power need to reckon with the increasingly emergent symbolic power of religion and its importance for the formation of the cultural consciousness and the collective identity of society. Since both politics and religion have to do with the order of the whole of the social lifeworld, they are in at least latent conflict. This is particularly the case for the monotheistic religions of Christianity and Islam, with their inherent universalist claims. In order that this conflict can take place in a way that preserves the freedom and the integrity of the partners, there needs to be a protected "public space" in which the debate about fundamental values can take place. For the sake of the viability and legitimacy of the social order, both religions and politics must work to ensure a certain fundamental consensus over regulatory principles that, as a framework of communicative power, can guide the processes of developing a legitimate legal order.

This study has gathered various examples from different contexts which show that religions have begun to engage in this way in the public sphere, in the framework of both political society and civil society. The interreligious dialogue that has been pursued intensively in recent decades at national and international level can be seen as a sign of the emerging "culture of dialogue and peace." In a world that is characterized by cultural and religious plurality, it is only when religions adapt themselves to a communicative relationship of dialogue that the necessary global dialogue about the basic rules of coexistence can begin.

This is especially the case for those countries and societies affected by conflicts over modernization. But we can draw the same conclusion when it comes to the global processes that aim at a new world order. The conditions for the creation of a "public space" at this level, however, exist even less than in the countries and regions that have been studied. It is true that in the meantime a network of civil society has developed at the global level. The statement of the former Brazilian president Fernando Cardoso as chair of the United Nations' "High Level Panel" supports the analysis in this study: "The power of civil society is a soft one. It is their capacity to argue, to propose, to experiment, to denounce, to be exemplary. It is not the power to decide. Such legitimacy is, by definition, a work in progress. It is never attained once and for all. It is gained in the arena of public debate and must be continually renewed and revitalized."[41] This panel has made proposals on how the impetus from the debate within civil society can be brought into the processes of political decision making at the intergovernmental level. There have been various suggestions that a permanent advisory body of representatives of religious and spiritual traditions could be created in the framework of the United Nations or of one of its specialized agencies such as UNESCO.[42]

However, does the specific contribution of the religions to the quest for a new world order really lie primarily in direct policy advice at the international level? Many of the major world religions already have consultative status at the Economic and Social Council through their specialized organizations. Too often, however, they succumb to the temptation to represent what are ultimately sectional institutional or political interests and thus to enter into competition with each other. The contribution of religions to create the global "public space" that is urgently required needs to be reflected in the efforts to clarify the ethical and moral foundations and the guiding principles of a new world order. If in the title of this section religions are described as "advocates for a culture of dialogue and peace," then this is more the description of a task than the role they are actually playing. But if Samuel Huntington's prediction of a "clash of civilizations" is to be refuted, then the religions are challenged to overcome friend-enemy thinking among their followers, and, in dialogue with each other, to mobilize the potential for peacemaking and reconciliation that exists in their traditions.

There are a plethora of approaches and initiatives for dialogue that are clarifying the ethical and moral foundations for a new world order. Religions are involved at the level of official representatives and experts. Yet few of the results and the insights that have been gained in these efforts have penetrated the awareness of the religions' adherents. If there is anything that distinguishes religious communities from the many other social groupings, however, it is the fact that they are rooted in the everyday lifeworld of their supporters right down to the smallest local communities. Through rituals, rules, symbols, stories, and teaching they influence the cultural awareness and the life of their followers, creating a space of solidarity and at the same time determining its borders. A culture of dialogue and peace will prevail only if it can be practiced in a "dialogue of life" in the everyday encounters between people and communities influenced by different cultural and religious traditions. This is especially important given the stresses and challenges for the coexistence of different communities that are related to the processes of cultural change resulting from conflicts over modernization. The change in awareness that is necessary needs to be promoted, above all, in and through religious communities.

Interreligious dialogue is at a critical stage. On the one hand, there are high expectations that the encounter of religions in dialogue could give a decisive boost to resolving global problems and the conflicts with which they are associated. On the other hand, there is increasing frustration that dialogue remains restricted to a limited group of official representatives and experts and provides little specific guidance in the search for "bridges of understanding" between exclusive identity claims of an ethno-national or cultural-religious nature.⁴³ Initiatives such as the "Declaration Toward a Global Ethic," the "Universal Declaration of Human Responsibilities," or the "Earth Charter" set out a vision, but the shift in consciousness that is anticipated is arrived at only slowly and often precisely in those situations of conflict in which the religious communities are required to act as advocates of a culture of dialogue and peace. To the extent that they themselves are able to build a foundation of mutual trust, they can open up the space in which social and political conflicts can be dealt with in dialogue and negotiations rather than confrontational debate.

Compared to the widely held view that the return of religion into the public space aggravates conflicts, the peacemaking potential that exists in all religions and thus their constructive public impact has been appreciated far too little. In 2007, Markus A. Weingardt, a staff member at the Global Ethic Foundation (*Stiftung Weltethos*), published a book on this very subject under the telling title: *Religion—Power—Peace: The Peace Potential of Religion in Violent Political Conflicts*.⁴⁴ Using six central case studies and 34 shorter examples he manages to demonstrate convincingly that in many of the well-known and lesser-known conflicts, religions and their leaders have played and continue to play an effective role in confidence building and the reduction of violence. Only in a few cases has religious mediation provided the crucial breakthrough for the peaceful resolution of conflict, but in many situations it was religiously motivated intervention that prepared the ground for subsequent political and diplomatic efforts to resolve the conflicts.

The crucial role of religions is primarily the task of reinstating communication that has broken down between the warring parties, and reducing distorted perceptions of the other side and their intentions. Because they usually enjoy greater confidence from the people and they are not normally accused of following their own political interests, they are often better than other mediators in being able to build the mutual trust that is necessary for the actual negotiations to resolve a dispute. Unlike the tendency of political actors to use ideology and religion to turn conflicts of interest and power into conflicts over fundamental values and identities, religious leaders, on account of their proximity to people's lives and expectations, attempt to trace back the conflicts over identity to the conflicting interests that are their roots and so to seek paths toward compromise.

As important as encouragement and support by partners from outside is, these examples show clearly that the ultimate potential for peace lies with the religious communities in the conflict regions themselves. Too great a solidarity from international organizations and religious networks can disrupt or even threaten the patient work of trust building in the situation itself. However, these examples also clearly demonstrate the importance of exchanging experiences in developing and deploying the peacemaking potential of religions. Forms of organization and networking that have proven themselves in one situation of conflict can provide assistance and impetus to efforts in other situations. In particular, we can see how important education among the members of religious communities can be in resisting the lure of radical positions. Religious communities in situations of conflict need to use persons whose moral authority is generally acknowledged to develop the skills of their members in building trust and mediation or arbitration.

Religions thus act as advocates for a culture of dialogue and peace to the extent that their relations with each other are guided by standards and principles such as those formulated in the "Declaration Toward a Global Ethic." Whereas the declaration sees the elements of the Global Ethic built on the "Golden Rule" as normative and unchangeable ethical precepts that are "convincing and practicable for all women and men of good will, religious and non-religious,"[45] in this study they are interpreted as "regulatory principles," rules for the necessary dialogue about how to promote a global order for decent life. In this dialogue all partners contribute their religious and ethical and moral traditions, their own culture and worldview. The principles contained in the Global Ethic Declaration, as well as in the other declarations that have been mentioned, do not take the place of the "thick" cultural-religious traditions in which the collective identity of a given human community is rooted. Instead, they create awareness that the various cultural and religious identities do not exclude each other but are linked together as expressions of a common humanity. Therefore, the rules can and should help in a process of mutual recognition and understanding of what contributes to the ordering of decent life. In this way they contribute to promoting the shift in consciousness that is needed. The viability of a new world order depends on whether and how it manages to communicate its principles and to "translate" them into the "language" of the different traditions. Only in this way will people in specific communities accept them as binding. This is a crucial task and is thereby the irreplaceable contribution of religions to building a new world order.

This distinctive role of religious communities and their leading representatives is put to the test especially in situations of conflict. Here, they have to demonstrate their moral and ethical credibility as advocates for a culture of dialogue and peace, which alone qualifies them for constructive conflict resolution or mediation. Such credibility will not automatically be given to religions and their leading representatives. It needs to be earned and it can be easily squandered, if religions disregard the critical demarcation line between political and religious action.

Summary and Conclusion

Thus we reach the conclusion of our explorations. This study has investigated the various ways of distinguishing between, or associating, religion and politics, from the secularist affirmation of the autonomy of politics and the simultaneous privatization of religion, to fundamentalist efforts to make religion the dominant factor of social order. Between these two extremes, there is a wide range of different historically and culturally conditioned forms of relationship. Both religion and politics have to do with the universal order of human society; they each represent different sources of power and are thus in latent tension with each other. In situations of cultural change, this tension can come into the open and force a renegotiation of the inherited forms of relationship. This applies to the relationship between religion and politics in individual countries and societies, but also in the search for a viable, decent human order of global coexistence of peoples and nations.

Particularly given the efforts to build a new world order, we demonstrated the need to transcend traditional concepts of the public order with their emphasis on the power of domination and the enforcing role of law, including the monopoly of violence, and to recognize the autonomous role of public religion for the foundation and legitimization of the social order. The distinction and the mutual association between political and religious activities must therefore be negotiated and take place in the public space, where the communicative power of a community is articulated in acts of lawmaking and their ethical and moral legitimacy. For the sake of the integrity of the autonomous contribution of religion and politics to shaping and maintaining the social order, we cannot dispense with the distinction between political and religious action, nor that between law and morality. The use of force or violence highlighted the critical limit. Politics in the form of state action cannot do without the coercive power of enforcement to maintain law and order. Religious action, however, makes use of symbolic, communicative power, expressed in the critical examination and reconnection of political action to the basic ethical and moral principles of order that express the fundamental consensus and the cultural and religious identity of society.

The distinction necessary to preserve the integrity of politics and religion was and is continually threatened by the claims of one side or the other to exert total control over the foundations and structures of social order. The tension that is thereby expressed between the power of politics and of religion cannot be eliminated by a complete separation of the two fields of action. Rather, they remain constitutively interrelated in their distinctiveness for the sake of the legitimacy of political action and the credibility of religion as guardians of cultural traditions. Especially in situations of cultural change, therefore, the relationship between politics and religion needs to be renegotiated, recognizing their different power potentials. Here there are no universally valid, normative criteria.

As far as the legitimacy of a new world order is concerned, a key priority was identified as creating and protecting a global public space, in which the interests of the people and nations are articulated rather than the national interests of the states, and in which a consensus is able to develop about the foundations of world order. This public space needs protection through "regulatory principles" that offer rules for the necessary dialogue between cultures and traditions. Religions as the guardians of the cultural traditions of their respective communities have an irreplaceable role in opening up their traditions in dialogue with each other and activating their inherent potential for the development of a common order and decent life. As advocates of a "culture of dialogue and peace," they can become trustees of the global public space. Thus they do not enter into competition with the tasks of politics but fulfil their role in the constitutive relatedness between religion and politics.

Notes

Introduction

1. Samuel P. Huntington, "The Clash of Civilizations?" *Foreign Affairs* 72, no. 3 (Summer 1993): 22–49; idem, *The Clash of Civilizations and the Remaking of World Order* (New York: Simon & Schuster, 1996).

2. Parliament of the World's Religions, "Declaration Toward a Global Ethic," 4 September 1993, http://www.weltethos.org/1-pdf/10-stiftung/declaration/declaration_english.pdf.

3. *Crossing the Divide: Dialogue among Civilizations* (South Orange, NJ : School of Diplomacy and International Relations, Seton Hall University, 2001).

4. http://www.weltethos.org/1-pdf/10-stiftung/declaration/declaration_english.pdf.

5. *Now Is the Time: Final Document and Other Texts*, World Convocation on Justice, Peace and the Integrity of Creation, Seoul, 1990 (Geneva: World Council of Churches, 1990), 11–21.

6. http://www.vatican.va/holy_father/benedict_xvi/encyclicals/documents/hf_ben-xvi_enc_20090629_caritas-in-veritate_en.html.

7. See Konrad Raiser, *For a Culture of Life: Transforming Globalization and Violence* (Geneva: WCC Publications, 2002).

CHAPTER 1: RELIGION AND POLITICS IN CONFLICT?

1. Cf. Thomas S. Axworthy, ed., *Bridging the Divide. Religious Dialogue and Universal Ethics, Papers for The InterAction Council* (Kingston, ON: McGill-Queens University Press, 2008).

2. Jan Assmann, *The Price of Monotheism*, trans. Robert Savage (Stanford: Stanford University Press, 2009), 15ff.; see also Peter Sloterdijk, *God's Zeal: The Battle of the Three Monotheisms* (Cambridge: Polity Press, 2009).

3. Ulrich Beck, *A God of One's Own: Religion's Capacity for Peace and Potential for Violence* (Cambridge: Polity Press, 2010), 54.

4. Rolf Schieder, *Sind Religionen gefährlich?* (Berlin: Berlin University Press, 2008), esp. 69ff.

5. Mark Juergensmeyer, *Terror in the Mind of God. The Global Rise of Religious Violence* (Berkeley: University of California Press, 2001); see also Schieder, *Religionen*, 24ff.

6. On the issue of religion and violence see also my essay, "Violence and Religion in Pluralistic Societies," in *The Orthodox Churches in a Pluralistic World: An Ecumenical Conversation*, ed. Emannuel Clapsis (Geneva/Brookline, MA: WCC Publications/Holy Cross Orthodox Press, 2004), 90–102.

7. Gilles Kepel, *The Revenge of God: Resurgence of Islam, Christianity, and Judaism in the Modern World* (Cambridge: Polity Press, 1994).

8. Jeff Haynes, *Religion in Global Politics* (London/New York: Pearson/Longman, 1998), 217.

9. Mark Juergensmeyer, *Global Rebellion: Religious Challenges to the Secular State, from Christian Militias to al Qaeda* (Berkeley: University of California Press, 2008), xi.

10. Ibid., 17.
11. Ibid., 21.
12. Ibid., 24.
13. Ibid., 26.
14. Ibid., 33.

15. Peter Beyer, *Religion and Globalization* (London: Sage, 1994), esp. 97ff.

16. Emile Durkheim, *The Elementary Forms of Religious Life* (New York: Oxford University Press, 2001), 41ff.

17. Theo Sundermeier, "Religion, Religionen," in *Lexikon Missionstheologischer Grundbegriffe*, ed. Karl Müller & Theo Sundermeier (Berlin: Reimer, 1987), 411.

18. Cf. Martin Riesebrodt, "Religion in Global Perspective," in *Global Religions: An Introduction*, ed. Mark Juergensmeyer (New York: Oxford University Press, 2003), 93ff; also Heinrich Schäfer, *Praxis—Theologie—Religion: Grundlinien einer Theologie- und Religionstheorie im Anschluss an Pierre Bourdieu* (Frankfurt am Main: Verlag Otto Lembeck, 2004), 261ff.

19. Stefan Huber, "Religion Monitor 2008: Structuring Principles, Operational Constructs, Interpretive Strategies," in *What the World Believes: Analysis and Commentary on the Religion Monitor 2008*, ed. Bertelsmann Stiftung (Gütersloh: Verlag Bertelsmann Stiftung, 2007), 19.

20. Riesebrodt, "Global Perspective," 100ff.

21. Schieder, *Religionen*, 40.

22. On this see Beyer, *Religion*, 5f.

23. Detlef Pollack, "Religion und Moderne. Religionssoziologische Erklärungsmodelle," in *Macht Glaube Politik?*, ed. Tobias Mörschel (Göttingen: Vandenhoeck & Ruprecht, 2006), 44.

24. Theo Sundermeier, *Religion was ist das?*, 2d ed. (Frankfurt/M: Verlag Otto Lembeck, 2007), 30.

25. Ibid., 40f.

26. Ibid., 41.

27. Ibid., 46.

28. Cf. Karl Jaspers, *The Origin and Goal of History*, new ed. (Abingdon, UK: Routledge, 2011).

29. Max Weber, "Politics as a Vocation," in *From Max Weber: Essays in Sociology*, ed. H. H. Gerth & C. Wright Mills (Abingdon, UK: Routledge, 1991), 77f.

30. Cf. Hannah Arendt, *The Human Condition*, 2d ed. (Chicago: University of Chicago Press, 1998); idem, *On Violence* (Orlando: Harcourt Brace, 1970).

31. Cf. Peter Bondanella and Mark Musa, eds., *The Portable Machiavelli* (New York: Viking Penguin, 1979).

32. Erhard Eppler, *Auslaufmodell Staat?* (Frankfurt/M: Suhrkamp Verlag, 2005), 162.

33. Cf. José Casanova, *Public Religions in the Modern World* (Chicago: University of Chicago Press, 1994), 61.

34. A general presentation of legal and social history can be found in Frank Crüsemann, *The Torah: Theology and Social History of Old Testament Law* (Edinburgh: T. & T. Clark, 1996).

35. On this see the more extensive discussion in chap. 5.

36. Cf. Max Weber, *Economy and Society* (Berkeley: University of California Press, 1968), 212ff., 399ff.

37. On this see Durkheim, *Elementary Forms*.

38. See Sundermeier, *Was ist das?*, 64.

39. Cf. Klaus Wengst, *Pax Romana: The Claim and the Reality* (London: SCM Press, 1987).

40. Hendrik Berkhof, *Kirche und Kaiser. Eine Untersuchung der Entstehung der byzantinischen und der theokratischen Staatsauffassung im vierten Jahrhundert* (Zollikon/Zürich: Evangelischer Verlag, 1947), 81f.

41. Ibid., 187.

42. Ibid., 212.

43. Otto Kallscheuer, "Macht Religion Politik? Ein Panorama," in Mörschel, *Macht*, 85.

44. Cf. Eugen Rosenstock-Huessy, *Out of Revolution: Autobiography of Western Man* (New York: Wm. Morrow, 1938).

45. Carlo Schmid, ed., *Machiavelli. Auswahl und Einleitung* (Frankfurt /Hamburg: Fischer-Verlag, 1956), 24.

46. Helmut Zeddies, *Bekenntnis als Einigungsprinzip* (Berlin: Evangelische Verlagsanstalt, 1980), 23.

47. Cf. Philip Benedict, "Religion and Politics in Europe, 1500–1700," in *Religion und Gewalt. Konflikte, Rituale, Deutungen*

(1500–1700), ed. Kaspar von Greyerz, et al. (Göttingen: Vandenhoeck & Ruprecht, 2006), 155–73.

48. The foundations of Durkheim's position are set out in his extensive research, *The Elementary Forms of Religious Life* (New York: Oxford University Press, 2008).

49. Max Weber, "Science as a Vocation," in Gerth and Mills, *From Max Weber*, 155.

50. Harvey Cox, *Religion in the Secular City: Toward a Postmodern Theology* (New York: Simon & Schuster, 1984), 19f.

51. Peter L. Berger, "The Desecularization of the World: A Global Overview," in idem., ed., *The Desecularization of the World: Resurgent Religion and World Politics* (Washington/Grand Rapids: Ethics and Public Policy Center/Eerdmans, 1999), 2.

52. Cf. Karel Dobbelare, *Secularization: An Analysis at Three Levels* (Brussels: PIE-Peter Lang, 2002).

53. Casanova, *Public Religions*, 19f.

54. José Casanova, "Beyond European and American Exceptionalism: towards a Global Perspective," in *Predicting Religion: Christian, Secular, and Alternative Futures*, ed. Grace Davie, et al. (Aldershot/Burlington: Ashgate, 2003), 22; cf. the study by David Martin, *On Secularization: Towards a Revised General Theory* (Aldershot/Burlington: Ashgate, 2005).

55. Cf. the research by Shmuel Eisenstadt, especially his programmatic essay, "Multiple Modernities," *Daedalus* 129, no. 1 (2000): 1–29.

56. Jürgen Habermas, "Faith and Knowledge," in idem, *The Future of Human Nature* (Cambridge: Polity Press, 1999), 104. For a critical discussion on the position of Habermas, see Thomas M. Schmidt, "The Discourse of Religion in the Post-Secular Society," in *Religion in the Public Sphere* (Bergen: Holberg Prize, 2005), 79–88, http://www.holbergprisen.no/images/materiell/2005_symposium_habermas.pdf.

57. Jürgen Habermas, "Religion in the Public Sphere," in ibid., 10–19.

58. Ibid., 18.

59. Grace Davie, *Europe: The Exceptional Case: Parameters of Faith in the Modern World* (London: Darton, Longman & Todd, 2002), 19.

Chapter 2: Beyond Church and State

1. Jürgen Habermas, *Between Facts and Norms: Contributions to a Discourse Theory of Law and Democracy* (Cambridge: MIT Press, 1996), 366f.

2. Ibid., 359f. (emphasis in original).

3. Ibid., 366 (emphasis in original).

4. Max Weber, *Economy and Society* (Berkeley: University of California Press, 1968), 54.

5. Cf. Hannah Arendt, *On Violence* (Orlando: Harcourt Brace, 1970), 35.

6. Cf. Gret Haller, *The Limits of Atlanticism: Perceptions of State, Nation and Religion in Europe and the United States* (Oxford: Berghahn Books, 2007).

7. Erhard Eppler, *Auslaufmodell Staat?* (Frankfurt/M: Suhrkamp Verlag, 2005), 47ff.

8. Arendt, *Violence*, 44.

9. Habermas, *Facts and Norms*, 150.

10. Ibid., 142.

11. José Casanova, *Public Religions in the Modern World* (Chicago: University of Chicago Press, 1994), 61.

12. Ibid., 228.

13. Ibid., 128f.

14. Mention can be made of the change in Roman Catholic positions on the role of the church in the political community, as expressed in the texts of the Second Vatican Council, especially the Declaration on Religious Freedom (*Dignitatis Humanae*) and the Pastoral Constitution on the Church in the Modern World (*Gaudium et Spes*), esp. para. 76, in Norman Tanner, *Vatican II: The Essential Texts* (New York: Image Books, 2012).

15. On this, see World Council of Churches, *Church and State: Opening a New Ecumenical Discussion*, Faith and Order Paper, no. 85 (Geneva: World Council of Churches, 1978).

16. Cf. Max Weber, "Churches and Sects in North America," in *The Protestant Ethic and the 'Spirit' of Capitalism and Other Writings*, ed. and trans. Peter Baehr and Gordon C. Wells (London: Penguin, 2002), 203–20; Ernst Troeltsch, *The Social Teaching of the Christian Churches*, vol. 1 (Louisville: Westminster John Knox, 1992), 328ff.

17. H. Richard Niebuhr, *The Social Sources of Denominationalism* (New York: Henry Holt, 1929), 18.

18. On the historical background to the separation of church and state in the United States, see Rainer Prätorius, *In God We Trust. Religion und Politik in den USA* (Munich: Beck, 2003), 31ff.

19. Robert N. Bellah, "Civil Religion in America," *Daedalus* 96, no. 1 (1966/7): 1–21.

20. Robert N. Bellah, *The Broken Covenant: American Civil Religion in Time of Trial* (New York: Seabury, 1975).

21. Casanova, *Public Religions*, 61.

22. Mark Juergensmeyer, *Global Rebellion: Religious Challenges to the Secular State, from Christian Militias to al Qaeda* (Berkeley: University of California Press, 2008), 9ff.

23. Cf. Theo Tschuy, *Ethnic Conflict and Religion: Challenge to the Churches* (Geneva: WCC Publications, 1997); also Heinrich Schäfer, "New Wars and Religious Identity Politics," in *Religions Today: Their Challenge to the Ecumenical Movement*, ed. Julio de Santa Ana (Geneva: WCC Publications, 2005), 89–104.

24. Cf. Jeff Haynes, *Religion in Global Politics* (New York: Pearson/Longman, 1998).

25. On this section see Ninan Koshy, *Religious Freedom in a Changing World* (Geneva: WCC Publications, 1992), 33ff., esp. 50.

Chapter 3: Religion and Politics in Islam

1. Organisation of Islamic Cooperation, *The Cairo Declaration on Human Rights in Islam*, http://www.oic-oci.org/english/article/human.htm.

2. Cf. Walid Saif, "Shari'ah and Modernity," in *Religion, Law and Society*, ed. Tarek Mitri (Geneva: WCC Publications, 1996), 11ff.; also: Ashgar Ali Engineer, "Tasbri' (process of Law-Making) in Islam," in Mitri, ed., *Religion, Law*, 33ff.

3. Cf. Hans Küng, *Islam: Past, Present, Future* (Oxford: Oneworld, 2007), 269ff.

4. Adel Theodor Khoury, "Das islamische Rechtssystem," in *Handbuch Recht und Kultur des Islams in der deutschen Gesellschaft*, ed. Adel Theodor Khoury, Peter Heine, Janbernd Oebbecke (Gütersloh: Gütersloher Verlagshaus, 2000), 48.

5. Hamid Enayat, *Modern Islamic Political Thought*, new ed. (London: I. B Taurus, 2005), 47; see also: Abodolkarim Soroush, "Shia Islam as a Factor in World Politics," in Thomas S. Axworthy, ed., *Bridging the Divide: Religious Dialogue and Universal Ethics, Papers for The InterAction Council* (Kingston, ON: McGill-Queens University Press, 2008), 87ff.

6. On the reform movements mentioned here and their main representatives, see Henning Wrogemann, *Missionarischer Islam und gesellschaftlicher Dialog* (Frankfurt/M: Verlag Otto Lembeck, 2006), 54ff.

7. For the description that follows, see esp. Enayat, *Islamic Political Thought*; also Heinrich Wilhelm Schäfer, *Kampf der Fundamentalismen. Radikales Christentum, radikaler Islam und Europas Moderne* (Frankfurt/M and Leipzig: Inseln-Verlag, 2008), esp. ch. 2, "Im Haus des Islam," 32–94.

8. For the history and significance of the Muslim Brotherhood and on the roles of Banna and Qutb, see Wrogemann, *Missionarischer Islam*, 94ff.

9. Cf. Schäfer, *Kampf*, 66ff.

10. Cf. here and for the following section, Said Amir Arjomand, "Islam," in *Global Religions: An Introduction*, ed. Mark Juergensmeyer (New York: Oxford University Press, 2003), 28ff.

11. Cf. Radwan Al-Sayyid, "Reform and Reconciliation between Religion and State. Some Trends in Contemporary Islam," in Julio de Santa Ana, ed., *Religions Today: Their Challenge to the Ecumenical Movement* (Geneva: WCC Publications, 2005), 189–209.

12. Abdullahi A. An-Na'im, "Political Islam in National Politics and International Relations," in Peter L. Berger, ed., *The Desecularization of the World: Resurgent Religion and World Politics* (Washington/Grand Rapids: Ethics and Public Policy Center/Eerdmans, 1999), 110.

13. Kamal Aboulmagd, "Islam as a Factor in Global Politics: Searching for Common Values to Guide a Globalizing World," in Axworthy, ed., *Bridging the Divide*, 104 (emphasis in original).

14. Abdullahi A. An-Naim, "Islamic Foundations of Religious Human Rights," in *Religious Human Rights in Global Perspective: Religious Perspectives*, vol. 1, ed. John Witte & Johan D. van der Vyver (The Hague: Marttnus Nijhof, 1996), 352.

15. Ibid., 348, 351.

16. Ibid., 353.

17. Ibid., 356.

18. Cf. ibid., 357.

19. An-Naim, "Political Islam," 120.

20. Mitri, *Religion, Law*; idem, *Religion and Human Rights: A Christian-Muslim Discussion* (Geneva: WCC Publications, 1996).

21. Mitri, ed., *Human Rights*, 11f.

22. *Striving Together in Dialogue: A Muslim-Christian Call to Reflection and Action* (Geneva: WCC Publications, 2001), http://www.oikoumene.org/en/resources/documents/wcc-programmes/interreligious-dialogue-and-cooperation/interreligious-trust-and-respect/striving-together-in-dialogue.html.

23. Ibid., 11f. (Nos. 31, 35).

24. "Reports of the three working groups from an international consultation on 'Christians and Muslims in Dialogue and Beyond,' in Geneva, October 16–18, 2002," *Current Dialogue* 40 (2002): 30–35.

25. Cited according to http://www.oikoumene.org/resources/documents/wcc-programmes/interreligious-dialogue-and-cooperation/interreligious-trust-and-respect/report-on-an-international-consultation-on-christians-and-muslims-in-dialogue-and-beyond.html.

26. Udo Steinbach, "Allianz gegen die Gewalt," in *welt-sichten* 4 (2009): 41ff.

27. *A Common Word between Us and You*, http://www.acommonword.com/index.php?lang=en&page=option1.

28. Ibid.

29. Steinbach, "Allianz," 43.

30. The Madrid Declaration issued by The World Conference on Dialogue, http://www.world-dialogue.org/Madrid/english/events/final.htm.

31. Ibid., 2 (No. 6).

32. Final Statement of Catholic-Muslim Forum, http://www.zenit.org/article-24175?l=english.

Chapter 4: The Challenge of Fundamentalism

1. Rainer Prätorius, *In God We Trust. Religion und Politik in den USA* (Munich: Beck, 2003), 14f.

2. J. Gresham Machen, *Christianity and Liberalism*, new ed. (Grand Rapids: Eerdmans, 1968); see also the extensive treatement of Machen in the essay of Miroslav Volf, "The Challenge of Protestant Fundamentalism," in *Fundamentalism as an Ecumenical Challenge*, ed. Hans Küng and Jürgen Moltmann, *Concilium* 3 (1992): 97ff.

3. See especially Meinrad Scherer-Emunds, *Die letzte Schlacht um Gottes Reich: Politische Heilsstrategien amerikanischer Fundamentalisten* (Münster: Edition Liberacion, 1989), 38ff.; also Heinrich Schäfer, *Protestantismus in Zentralamerika* (Frankfurt/M: Peter Lang, 1992), 49ff.

4. For a historical analysis of the complicated relationships between evangelicals and fundamentalists see: George Marsden, "From Fundamentalism to Evangelicalism: A Historical Analysis," in *The Evangelicals: What They Believe, Who They Are, Where They Are Changing*, ed. David F. Wells and John D. Woodbridge (Nashville: Abingdon, 1975), 122ff.; see also, in the same volume, Martin E. Marty, "Tensions within Contemporary Evangelicalism: A Critical Appraisal," 170ff.; and George H. Williams and Rodney L. Peterson, "Evangelicals: Society, the State, the Nation (1925–75)," 211ff.

5. For a more detailed analysis see: José Casanova, *Public Religions in the Modern World* (Chicago: University of Chicago Press, 1994), 145ff.; Jeff Haynes, *Religion in Global Politics* (London/New York: Pearson/Longman, 1998), 28ff; Peter Beyer, *Religion and Globalization* (London: Sage, 1994), 114ff; Prätorius, *In God We Trust*, 112ff., 164ff.; and Josef Braml, "Das politische Erfolgskonzept der Christlichen Rechten in den USA: Vom fundamentalistischen Sektierertum zum politischen Pragmatismus," in *Macht Glaube Politik?*, ed. Tobias Mörschel (Göttingen: Vandenhoeck & Ruprecht, 2006), 165ff.

6. Braml, "Erfolgskonzept," 173.

7. For a more extensive treatment see Casanova, *Public Religions*, 149ff.; on the self-portrayal of religious conservatives as "victims" of allegedly dominant "secular humanism," see also Rainer Prätorius, "Religiöse Politik und politisierte Religion in den USA," in Mörschel, ed., *Macht*, 158ff.

8. See the analysis of Prätorius, *Trust*, 116ff; also Tarek Mitri, *Au nom de la Bible. Au nom de Amerique* (Geneva: Labor et Fides, 2004), esp. ch. 3; idem, *Im Namen Gottes? Politik und Religion in den USA* (Frankfurt/M: Verlag Otto Lembeck, 2005).

9. On this see Martin Marty, "What is Fundamentalism? Theological Perspectives," in Küng and Moltmann, eds., *Fundamentalism*, 3ff.

10. See above, p. 97.

11. John Coleman, "Global Fundamentalism: Sociological Perspectives," in Küng and Moltmann, *Fundamentalism*, 38f.

12. Heinrich Wilhelm Schäfer, *Kampf der Fundamentalismen. Radikales Christentum, radikaler Islam und Europas Moderne* (Frankfurt/M and Leipzig: Inseln-Verlag, 2008), 18.

13. Ibid., 19f.

14. Ibid., 21.

15. Cf. Gilles Kepel, *The War for Muslim Minds: Islam and the West* (Cambridge: Harvard University Press, 2004), 137.

16. Cf. Schäfer, *Kampf*, 67f.

17. For an extensive presentation see Mark Juergensmeyer, *Global Rebellion: Religious Challenges to the Secular State, from Christian Militias to al Qaeda* (Berkeley: University of California Press, 2008), 43ff.

18. Schäfer, *Kampf*, 70.

19. See the studies by Hamid Enayat, *Modern Islamic Political Thought*, new ed. (London: I. B. Taurus, 2005), 160ff.; Beyer, *Religion*, 160ff.; also Schäfer, *Kampf*, 71ff.; also Juergensmeyer, *Global Rebellion*, 46ff.

20. Schäfer, *Kampf*, 73.

21. On this section see Beyer, *Religion*, 185ff.

22. Cf. Juergensmeyer, *Global Rebellion*, 54ff.

23. On this section see Haynes, *Global Politics*, 168ff.; also Juergensmeyer, *Global Rebellion*, 103ff.

24. Schäfer, *Kampf*, 96.

25. See above, p. 64.

26. Casanova, *Public Religions*, 157.

27. Ibid., 165f.

Chapter 5: Religion, Power, and Politics

1. Max Weber, "Politics as a Vocation," in *From Max Weber: Essays in Sociology*, ed. H. H. Gerth & C. Wright Mills (Abingdon, UK: Routledge, 1991), 77f.

2. Erhard Eppler, *Auslaufmodell Staat?* (Frankfurt/M: Suhrkamp Verlag, 2005), 75.

3. Max Weber, *Economy and Society* (Berkeley: University of California Press, 1968), 53.

4. Ibid., 215.

5. Paul Tillich, "The State as Expectation and Demand," in idem, *Political Expectation* (New York: Harper & Row, 1971), 99.

6. Ibid.

7. Weber, "Politics," 78.

8. Hannah Arendt, *On Violence* (Orlando: Harcourt Brace, 1970).

9. Ibid., 41.

10. Ibid., 42.

11. Ibid., 44.

12. Hannah Arendt, *The Human Condition*, 2d ed. (Chicago: University of Chicago Press, 1998), 200.

13. Arendt, *Violence*, 51f.

14. Ibid., 56.

15. Cf. Hannah Arendt, *Macht und Gewalt* (Munich: Piper, 1970), 58.

16. See, for example, Peter M. Blau, *Exchange and Power in Social Life* (New York: Wiley, 1964; new ed., New Brunswick: Transaction, 1986); Dennis Wrong, *Power: Its Forms, Bases, and Uses* (New York: Harper & Row, 1979; new ed., New Brunswick: Transaction, 1995); Antje Vollmer, *Heißer Frieden. Über Gewalt, Macht und Zivilisation* (Munich: DTV, 1995); Angus Stewart, *Theories of Power and Domination* (London: Sage, 2001).

17. Weber, *Economy*, 34.

18. Cf. Wrong, *Power*, 2; Blau, *Exchange*, 222.

19. Carl Friedrich von Weizsäcker, *Die Zeit drängt* (Munich: Carl Hanser Verlag, 1986), 63.

20. Cf. Jürgen Habermas, *Between Facts and Norms: Contributions to a Discourse Theory of Law and Democracy* (Cambridge: MIT Press, 1996), esp. 132ff., 329ff.

21. Ibid., 147f.

22. Ibid., 150.

23. Cf. Weber, *Economy*; Habermas, *Facts and Norms*.

24. Cf. Wolfgang Huber, *Gerechtigkeit und Recht, Grundlinien einer christlichen Rechtsethik* (Gütersloh: Gütersloher Verlagshaus, 1996), esp. 52ff.

25. Ibid., 41.

26. Cited according to Sean MacBride, "The Rule of Law: A Basis of Responsible Society," in Z. K. Matthews, *Responsible Government in a Revolutionary Age* (New York: Association/London: SCM, 1966), 251.

27. U.N. General Assembly, "Universal Declaration of Human Rights," 10 December 1948, http://www.un.org/en/documents/udhr/.

28. Baas de Gaay Fortman und Berma Klein Goldewijk, *Where Needs Meet Rights: Economic, Social, and Cultural Rights in a New Perspective* (Geneva: WCC Publications, 1999).

29. On this, see Geneviève Jacques, *Resisting the Intolerable* (Geneva: WCC Publications, 2007), 32ff.

30. Wolfgang Huber, *Violence: The Unrelenting Assault on Human Dignity*, trans. Ruth C. L. Gritsch (Minneapolis: Fortress Press, 1996), 125; cf. idem, *Gerechtigkeit*, 233; on the issue of human rights as a whole, 225–33. For a discussion in English see also idem, "Human Rights and Biblical Legal Thought," in *Religious Human Rights in Global Perspective: Religious Perspectives*, vol. 1, ed. John Witte and Johan D. van der Vyver (The Hague: Marttnus Nijhof, 1996), 47–63.

31. Cf. chap. 3 above, 63–64.

32. Huber, *Gerechtigkeit*, 267, 372ff.; cf. idem, "Human Rights," 63.

33. See Dieter Conrad, *Gandhi und der Begriff des Politischen: Staat, Religion und Gewalt* (Munich: Wilhem Fink Verlag, 2006), 95ff.

34. The concept of "communicative action" is used here as in the analysis of Dieter Conrad, who based himself on Jürgen Habermas's distinction between "strategic" and "communicative" action; *Gandhi*, 105f.

35. Ibid., 108.

36. Ibid., 110.

37. Cf. ch. 1 above, 38.

38. See Michael Walzer, *Thick and Thin: Moral Argument at Home and Abroad* (Notre Dame, IN: University of Notre Dame Press, 1994).

39. Parliament of the World's Religions, "Declaration Toward a Global Ethic," 4 September 1993, http://www.weltethos.org/1-pdf/10-stiftung/declaration/declaration_english.pdf.

40. See my essay, "Global Order and Global Ethic," in *In Search of Universal Values*, ed. Karl-Josef Kuschel and Dietmar Mieth, *Concilium* 4 (2001): 19–24.

41. High Level Panel on UN-Civil Society, "Civil Society and Global Governance," contextual paper prepared by the panel's chairman Fernando Henrique Cardoso, http://www.un-ngls.org/orf/ecosoc%20HL%20Panel%20-%20Contextual%20paper%20by%20Mr%20Cardoso%20Chairman.doc.

42. Such an agreement has in the meantime been made between the Director General of UNESCO and a high-level group of religious leaders on 22 July 2009 in Moscow.

43. See the report of a World Council of Churches' conference in 2005 on the theme "Critical Moment in Interreligious Relations and Dialogue," in Hans Ucko, ed., *Changing the Present, Dreaming the Future. A Critical Moment in Interreligious Dialogue* (Geneva: WCC Publications, 2006).

44. Markus A. Weingardt, *Religion Macht Frieden. Das Friedenspotential von Religionen in politischen Gewaltkonflikten* (Stuttgart: Verlag W. Kohlhammer, 2007).

45. Parliament of the World's Religions, "Declaration Toward a Global Ethic," 4 September 1993, Chicago, http://www.weltethos.org/1-pdf/10-stiftung/declaration/declaration_english.pdf, 6.